Embracing Accountability

A Supervisor's Guide to Driving Results

Dr. Patrick C. Patrong

Embracing Accountability

A Supervisor's Guide to
Driving Results

Dr. Patrick C. Patrong

President/CEO
Patrong Enterprises, Inc.

Richmond, VA

Embracing Accountability: A Supervisor's Guide to Driving Results

For information regarding permissions or speaking engagements, contact:
Patrong Enterprises, Inc.

Richmond, Virginia   Telephone/WhatsApp: 1.410.294.5431
Website: www.patrong.com   Email: info@patrong.com

All examples, case studies, and scenarios in this book are inspired by real organizational settings but are presented in a composite form to preserve confidentiality and learning value. Names, roles, and details have been altered.

Printed in the United States of America.

ISBN: 979-8-9998411-2-4

Library of Congress Control Number: *Pending*

Design and Layout: Patrong Enterprises, Inc. **Cover Design:** "PEI Creative Studio 1A

First Edition: 2025

Legal Disclaimer
This publication is intended to provide general leadership and supervisory guidance. It is not intended to substitute for legal, human resources, or compliance advice tailored to any specific organization. Readers should consult their agency or legal counsel before applying any policies or procedures discussed in this book.

DEDICATION

To the leaders who taught me that accountability begins long before the challenge — and to those who continue to hold me to the same standard. Your lessons shaped this work.

To the men and women of public service who stand tall in the quiet work of responsibility. You are the unseen foundation of excellence, integrity, and trust.

And to every supervisor learning that accountability is not about control but about care — may you lead with clarity, consistency, and character, transforming your team one conversation at a time.

CONTENTS

ACCOUNTABILITY STEWARDSHIP BEFORE THE CHALLENGE

Supervisors Must Step Forward First

Introduction

Accountability. It is a word that can inspire confidence or trigger unease. For some, it signals ownership, clarity, and pride in delivering results. For others, it carries the weight of blame, punishment, and finger-pointing. In truth, accountability is neither friend nor foe — it is a force. How supervisors choose to utilize it will determine whether it strengthens or weakens their teams.

This book, Embracing Accountability: A Supervisor's Guide to Driving Results, is about reclaiming accountability as a positive, proactive practice. Rather than something to fear when things go wrong, accountability can become the steady hand that keeps programs, people, and public trust on course. It is not about punishment; it is about stewardship.

I wrote this book because supervisors — especially those in state and municipal organizations — occupy a unique position. You are the bridge between policy and practice, between leaders who come and go and the employees who remain, between community expectations and organizational realities. When a program succeeds, supervisors are rarely celebrated. When a program falters, supervisors often stand in the spotlight. That reality can make accountability feel like a burden. However, with the right mindset and tools, accountability can become a source of credibility, influence, and stability.

Inside these chapters, you will discover how to:

- Redefine accountability from punishment to ownership.

- Model accountability as stewardship in anticipation of the challenge.

- Shape beliefs and experiences that create a culture of responsibility.

- Set standards and communicate them in a way that is clear and effective.

- Utilize tools and systems to ensure accountability is transparent and fair.

- Coach employees toward growth while maintaining high expectations.

- Sustain accountability even in unionized, politically sensitive, or highly regulated environments.

Each chapter is designed to be read in one sitting. You will find public sector case snapshots drawn from real challenges supervisors face. You will see the applied tools you can put to use immediately. You will be prompted by reflection questions that make the concepts personal. Furthermore, you will close each chapter with a leadership-centered summary and an original quote to anchor the lesson.

You will also encounter what I call "Magic with a Message." These are simple illusions I use in training to make abstract concepts memorable. They remind us that leadership is not only about information but also about imagination — finding ways to make truths stick. Whether it is rope, water, or paper, the trick always points back to a principle: leadership that embraces accountability creates the conditions for others to succeed.

The chapters ahead will challenge you, but they will also equip you. Accountability is not a destination; it is a daily practice. By the end of this book, you will have a new lens through which to see your role as a supervisor — not as one who reacts to failure, but as one who claims responsibility before the challenge and leads your team with clarity, courage, and care.

So let us begin. The first step in embracing accountability is redefining it — not as a shadow that follows failure, but as the light that guides success.

"Accountability is the hand a leader raises before the storm; it steadies the team and signals that failure will be met with remedy, not retribution." — Dr. Patrick C. Patrong.

Accountability as Stewardship Before the Challenge

Why Supervisors Must Step Forward First

Accountability is often misunderstood as a backward-looking action: a response to failure, a mechanism for sanction, or a tool for assigning blame. In practice, organizations treat accountability like a rear-view mirror. They examine the damage, trace the trajectory, and then try to find the cause. That model is costly. It wastes time, corrodes trust, and incentivizes concealment rather than candid problem-solving. There is a different and far more powerful way to practice accountability — as stewardship in anticipation of the challenge. When supervisors claim ownership at the outset of a program or initiative, they alter the team's psychology, the stakeholders' expectations, and the organization's ability to withstand political or operational turbulence.

To claim stewardship is to say, explicitly and publicly, "I own the outcome and I will lead the work to get us there." That sentence shifts many of the assumptions that drive daily behavior. People who work under a steward do not ask, "Who will get blamed?" They ask, "How can I contribute?" They do not hide problems; they report them earlier because they believe early disclosure will result in help, not punishment. The practical result of proactive stewardship is a team that is anticipatory, resilient, and collaborative.

Magic with a Message brings this idea to life in tangible form. In workshops, I use a simple sealed envelope illusion. I place a small object into a sealed envelope at the beginning of the session and later reveal that it has transformed or appeared in a new place. The trick illustrates a single point: what you place into the process at the beginning determines what you reveal at the end. If you establish ownership and clarity from the outset, the outcome is more likely to be integrity and valuable results. If you place avoidance and ambiguity, expect confusion and compromised outcomes. That metaphor is not theatrical — it is managerial truth.

Redefining Accountability: Ownership, Not Punishment

Accountability's reputation for punishment is deserved only insofar as leaders allow it to be used that way. When accountability becomes synonymous with discipline, it produces two predictable behaviors: cover-up and compliance. Cover-up occurs because employees fear the consequences of being honest. Compliance occurs because people focus on avoiding punishment rather than pursuing value. Neither serves organizational performance.

Redefining accountability as ownership starts with language and is solidified by consistent behavior. The words supervisors choose matter. "Who is to blame?" prompts a search for a scapegoat. "Who owns this outcome?" prompts problem ownership. "Why didn't this happen?" invites rationalizations. "How do we secure success?" closes on solutions. Language changes mental framing; framing changes responses.

The second element is visibility. A supervisor who claims ownership must visibly organize, resource, and monitor the work. Ownership without action is hollow. The leader who publicly commits to a result and then sets milestones, meetings, and supports for the team creates predictable patterns. People say what they know; they escalate problems early; they contribute practical solutions instead of defensive explanations. Over time, visible stewardship converts suspicion into trust.

The Supervisor's Practical Role: Define, Map, Declare

Proactive accountability is practical. It consists of three repeated actions that supervisors must perform before a program launches: defining success, mapping risks, and declaring ownership.

Define success. Vague goals allow blame to be diffused. Specific, measurable outcomes make accountability fair and actionable. Instead of "improve service," define "reduce average wait times by 20% within six months." Instead of "increase outreach," define "add 10 community pop-ups and measure attendance." Clarity about outcomes gives people a target and reduces ambiguity about what constitutes success versus failure.

Map risks. Identify what can derail the effort and describe how you will notice early signals. Consider vendor reliability, staffing pinch points, political interventions, or public relations risks. For each risk, write the early signals you would see — an increase in canceled appointments, late vendor confirmations, a surge in social media complaints — and the proactive steps you will take to reduce the likelihood or the impact. This mapping is not pessimism; it is stewardship.

Declare ownership. The declaration must be public, specific, and placed it in the project charter. Speak it at the kick-off. Write it in the weekly agenda. The phrase does not need to be grandiose; it needs to be visible. "I will be accountable for the client portal rollout," followed immediately by details on checkpoints and supports, is more credible than an abstract promise. The supervisor who declares ownership early establishes a single person or role to which accountability coheres — the organization has a focal point that others may rely on.

Shaping Beliefs and Experiences: Beyond Policies to Culture

Accountability is cultural at its core. Policies and procedures are necessary but insufficient. Culture Partners' Results Pyramid (experiences → beliefs → actions → results) is an instructive model: to produce different results, you must design different experiences that shift beliefs and, in turn, actions.

Experiences are the events and rituals that people live through within an organization. The opening meetings of an initiative, the tone of communications, the rituals of recognition — these create immediate experiences that scaffold beliefs. If a new initiative begins with a defensive memo and last-minute directives, the experience teaches people that accountability means blame. If a new initiative begins with a public declaration of stewardship, scheduled support sessions, and clear learning checkpoints, the experience teaches people that accountability means shared responsibility.

Beliefs are the internal narratives people carry: "If I speak up, I will be supported" versus "If I speak up, I will be blamed." Leaders shape those narratives through consistent behavior. When leaders repeatedly respond to early problem reports with coaching and resources rather than punishment, they change the belief landscape. Over time, this shift produces different actions: early reporting, collaborative problem-solving, and collective ownership.

The mistake leaders often make is assuming that checklists create culture. They do not. Checklists are helpful tools, but they must be coupled with deliberate experiences that teach and reinforce the kind of behavior the organization needs. Designing those experiences — the weekly accountability rhythm, the transparent decision log, the public milestone celebrations — is part of the supervisor's stewardship.

Accountability Before the Challenge: Why it Matters in the Public Sector

Supervisors in state and municipal roles face distinctive realities that amplify the importance of proactive stewardship. First, public organizations operate in visible spaces. Program failures not only affect service users but can rapidly become political problems. Second, supervisors and career staff often outlast elected officials and changing administrations. Third, unions, procurement rules, and regulatory constraints complicate the path from plan to execution.

In such contexts, claiming accountability before the challenge is a stabilizing force. When a supervisor publicly declares ownership and documents plans and risks, it becomes easier to preserve continuity across political transitions. When a program is structured around clear, documented stewardship, new leaders can see the logic and the safeguards and are less likely to cancel or undermine valuable services. The proactive supervisor builds institutional memory and operational credibility.

Public Sector Case Snapshot: Angela's Vaccination Outreach

Scene 1 — The Mandate

Angela was a mid-level county health supervisor tasked with designing and implementing a neighborhood vaccination outreach program within six months. The directive came from political leadership, and the community was watching. Funding lines were ambiguous, and vendor details were provisional. Staff were committed but stretched. Many in her position might have convened a planning meeting and circulated a memo. Angela did something different: she publicly declared, at the initial cross-departmental meeting, "I will be accountable for ensuring this program reaches our residents. We will document decisions, report weekly, and adapt as needed."

Scene 2 — The Risk Map

She organized the team around a risk map. To address supply chain vulnerabilities, she initiated secondary vendor agreements. To address community mistrust, she developed public messaging in collaboration with local nonprofits. For staffing, she established a volunteer pool and cross-training schedule. For political risk, she invited a liaison from the county administrator's office to receive weekly written updates and offered a transparent briefing schedule to elected officials. Her map was explicit and visible.

Scene 3 — Early Setback

Three months in, a primary vendor delayed shipments. A local influencer began circulating misleading information on social platforms. Instead of surprise or panic, Angela convened the weekly accountability meeting — the one she had scheduled in the charter — and presented the vendor status, the rapid response messaging, and an alternative staffing plan for pop-up sites. She asked the team for solutions and recognized those who volunteered additional shifts. The early transparency helped reduce rumors and facilitated faster corrective action.

Scene 4 — Political Transition

An election brought a new leadership team to the county. Instead of scrapping the program, the new administration reviewed the project documentation and saw Angela's public commitment, regular updates, and the evidence of outcome tracking. They elected to continue the program and authorized a modest supplemental budget. The program continued, adapted, and ultimately exceeded its outreach targets.

Scene 5 — The Outcome and the Lesson

At the end of the first cycle, the initiative had reached more residents than projected, community satisfaction rose, and staff reported higher confidence in delivering services. The achievement was not that no problems occurred; problems did occur. The achievement was that when problems occurred, the team solved them publicly, with documented steps and visible leadership. Angela's upfront stewardship established a predictable and durable pathway to results.

Applied Tool: The Proactive Accountability Map

The Proactive Accountability Map is a single-page tool supervisors can use to transform aspiration into operational stewardship. Use it for any initiative.

Step 1 — Define the initiative in one sentence and specify the scope. (Example: Neighborhood Vaccination Outreach — six zip codes, pop-up clinics, mobile unit support.)

Step 2 — List 2–3 measurable success metrics. (Example: +20% clinic attendance; 15% of the target population reached; 80% community satisfaction.)

Step 3 — Identify stakeholders and dependencies. (Example: county procurement, vendor, nonprofits, clinics, elected office.)

Step 4 — Map likely risks and early warning signals. (Example: shipment delays — vendor ALT flags; misinformation — spike in social mentions.)

Step 5 — Record proactive actions you will take now (before the risk appears). (Example: secure secondary vendor, pre-draft messaging, cross-train staff.)

Step 6 — Publicly declare stewardship in the charter and establish a schedule for accountability checkpoints (e.g., weekly or biweekly). (Example: weekly 45-minute standing meeting, public updates to stakeholders.)

Step 7 — Document decisions, learning, and adjustments in a shared log after each checkpoint.

Worked Example — Applying the Map to Angela's program

Initiative: Neighborhood Vaccination Outreach — Scope: six zip codes, pop-up clinics, mobile unit support.

Success Metrics: +20% clinic attendance; 15% of the target population reached; 80% community satisfaction.

Stakeholders: County public health, local clinics, nonprofits, vendors, and elected office holders.

Likely Risks & Signals: shipment delays (vendor alerts), misinformation (social mentions spike), staffing shortages (appointment cancellations).

Proactive Actions: secure secondary vendor agreements now; pre-draft social messaging and rapid response plan; cross-train staff and recruit volunteers.

Declaration & Cadence: project charter with public ownership statement; weekly accountability meetings; published progress updates to stakeholders.

When supervisors use this map, they create a durable paper trail for decisions and encourage early problem reporting — both of which reduce political and operational exposure.

Coaching with Accountability: The Balance of High Standards and Human Support

Accountability asserted early does not absolve supervisors from coaching or soften expectations — it reframes correction as part of ongoing development and growth. The distinction between coaching and discipline is crucial. Coaching begins with curiosity and data. Start by asking for context: "Help me understand what happened." Pair that with clear standards and an action plan: "Here is the gap and here is how we bridge it." Finally, agree on support and timelines. That pattern signals that accountability is not a trap but a pathway for improvement.

Supervisors also must plan for capacity. Expectations without resources produce cynicism. Demonstrate stewardship by ensuring staff have training, reasonable timelines, and recognition for effort. Cross-training, documented backup plans, and scheduled relief reduce burnout and make accountability sustainable.

Reflection Questions

1. How do I explicitly define accountability in my role — as ownership or punishment? Name an example where your language conveyed one or the other and how you would change it.

2. Choose one current or upcoming initiative. What would your public stewardship declaration be? Write the exact sentence you will use and the forum where you will deliver it.

3. Identify three likely risks for that initiative. For each risk, name one proactive action you will take today to reduce the probability or impact.

4. What cadence of accountability checkpoints will you use? Will it be weekly, biweekly, or monthly — and what will be the standing agenda?

5. What supports do your staff need to accept ownership safely? Consider training, time, recognition, and psychological safety measures.

Leadership-Centered Closing Summary

Accountability is most potent when it is claimed before the challenge. Supervisors who act as stewards change the default behaviors of teams: people report early, solve problems collaboratively, and sustain programs through political or operational turbulence. This behavior is not rhetorical idealism; it is practical leadership. When you declare ownership publicly, map risks, and put supports in place, you institutionalize decision-making that outlives any single leader.

"The most powerful accountability is the kind that is claimed before the challenge, not assigned after the crisis."

— Dr. Patrick C. Patrong

"Leaders who raise their hand early to own results rarely have to point their finger later." — Dr. Patrick C. Patrong

Final Charge

This week, pick one active or upcoming program and complete a Proactive Accountability Map for it. Publish a short stewardship statement in your next team meeting. Schedule your first accountability checkpoint. Accountability is a habit, not a slogan. Start by practicing it before the challenge arrives, and your team will be better prepared when it does.

UNDERSTANDING THE ACCOUNTABILITY MINDSET

Introduction — Mindset Shapes Outcomes

Before accountability is expressed in policies, performance reviews, or project updates, it is formed in the mind. A supervisor's mental model of accountability determines how it is practiced and how employees experience it. When supervisors view accountability primarily as enforcement, they often create an atmosphere of fear and compliance. When they view it as stewardship, they create an atmosphere of growth and trust.

The challenge is that mindsets are invisible but powerful. They act like the lens in a pair of glasses: everything you see is colored by them, often without you noticing. To embrace accountability, supervisors must first examine their own lens. Are you approaching accountability as a blame-seeker, a box-checker, or a steward? Each mindset produces different outcomes.

In this chapter, we explore what it means to cultivate an accountability mindset. We examine how to shift from blame to responsibility, how to foster proactive and growth-oriented thinking, and how to overcome common barriers that keep accountability trapped in negativity. Along the way, we will examine public-sector realities, explore how beliefs and behaviors intersect, and acquire practical strategies to transform our thinking so that accountability becomes empowering rather than intimidating.

Section 1 — From Blame to Responsibility

Blame is often the reflexive response when something goes wrong in an organization. A project runs behind schedule, a public service fails to meet expectations, or a compliance audit highlights gaps, and the instinct is to ask: "Who is at fault?" This question feels natural because it promises relief — if we can locate the guilty party, then perhaps the rest of us are safe. However, blame rarely produces improvement. It creates fear, fuels defensiveness, and encourages employees to hide problems rather than address and resolve them.

In supervisory roles, especially in the public sector, the blame game can be particularly destructive. Citizens expect transparency, political leaders demand explanations, and unions or employee associations scrutinize every disciplinary action. When supervisors respond to mistakes by casting blame, they not only discourage candid dialogue but also expose themselves and their organizations to mistrust and prolonged conflict. What may feel like a quick way to "show accountability" often backfires, leaving programs weakened and teams demoralized.

Responsibility is a more effective alternative. Where blame seeks culprits, responsibility seeks causes and solutions. A supervisor who embraces responsibility asks: "What in the system allowed this failure? What can I do, as the leader, to prevent it from happening again?" This shift requires humility. It asks leaders to admit that oversight, resources, training, or clarity may have been lacking. However, it also models courage, as it signals that the supervisor is not afraid to stand in the gap and take ownership of the outcome.

When supervisors model responsibility, employees notice. Instead of bracing for punishment, they lean in with ideas. Instead of hiding mistakes, they disclose them early. Responsibility fosters a climate in which problems are addressed before they escalate into crises. Moreover, in environments where scrutiny is constant — such as city councils, state legislatures, and oversight boards — a culture of early disclosure can mean the difference between a minor setback and a headline-grabbing scandal.

Magic with a Message: The "Professor's Nightmare" illusion — three ropes of different lengths that transform into equal lengths — illustrates this shift beautifully. At first glance, the ropes appear unequal. Blame sees those differences as justification for unequal treatment. Responsibility, however, is the act of aligning people to the same standard, regardless of their starting point. The illusion shows that what feels impossible is possible with the right mindset: supervisors can create fairness where others expect only inequity.

Consider the story of a transportation supervisor who inherited a bus fleet plagued with maintenance delays. His predecessor blamed mechanics for being "lazy." Instead of repeating this narrative, the new supervisor accepted responsibility for it. He reviewed schedules, discovered that spare parts were ordered through a cumbersome procurement system, and worked with city leadership to streamline the process. He also invested in training so mechanics could anticipate problems instead of waiting for breakdowns. Within a year, fleet availability improved by 25 percent. The mechanics had not been lazy; they had been trapped in a broken system. By shifting from blame to responsibility, the supervisor unlocked solutions that blame had obscured.

The principle is clear: blame looks backward, responsibility looks forward. Blame isolates individuals, responsibility strengthens teams. Blame protects egos, responsibility protects outcomes. In assuming responsibility, supervisors model the very accountability they expect from their teams — not by pointing fingers, but by extending a hand.

"Accountability with a growth mindset is not about catching people failing; it is about helping people grow strong enough to succeed."

— Dr. Patrick C. Patrong

Section 2 — Developing a Growth-Oriented Mindset

Accountability without growth is nothing more than surveillance. When supervisors focus only on catching mistakes **or** enforcing rules, they create a culture of compliance — employees do just enough to avoid negative attention. Nevertheless, in a world where public needs are constantly evolving, compliance alone is insufficient. Supervisors must nurture growth, and this begins with mindset.

A growth-oriented accountability mindset reframes mistakes as opportunities for growth. Instead of asking, "Who failed?" supervisors ask, "What did we learn?" This shift does not lower standards; it raises them by insisting that every outcome, good or bad, contributes to improvement. Employees who see their supervisors respond to mistakes with curiosity and coaching rather than condemnation become more resilient. They are willing to try, fail, and try again — which is how innovation happens.

The research of psychologist Carol Dweck on the growth mindset provides powerful insight here. Dweck found that individuals who believe abilities can be developed through effort and learning are more persistent, more adaptable, and more engaged. Supervisors who internalize this research understand that accountability is not about catching employees in failure but about developing them toward success.

In practical terms, supervisors with a growth-oriented mindset respond differently in everyday situations. When an employee misses a deadline, the punitive supervisor thinks, "They are unreliable." The growth-oriented supervisor thinks, "Did I provide the right tools? What can we adjust so this does not happen again?" When an employee struggles with a new policy, the supervisor often blames the employee's incompetence. The growth-oriented supervisor considers whether more explicit guidance or additional training might be required. Over time, this mindset produces a workforce that sees challenges as solvable rather than threatening.

This approach is particularly critical in state and municipal settings. Unlike private sector firms, which can often pivot quickly or allocate additional resources to address problems, public-sector organizations operate under constraints: fixed budgets, strict procurement processes, and constant public scrutiny. A growth-oriented mindset enables supervisors to transform those constraints into opportunities. Limited budgets encourage creative use of existing resources. Rigid regulations encourage process discipline. Public scrutiny encourages transparency. When accountability is practiced through a growth lens, obstacles become catalysts for improvement.

Magic with a Message: One illusion I often perform involves pouring water into a newspaper. Audiences expect the paper to become soggy and fall apart — but when the paper is opened, it is dry, and the water is gone. The point is simple: what you expect does not have to determine what is possible. The same is true of accountability. If supervisors expect accountability to destroy morale, it will. Nevertheless, if they expect accountability to reveal hidden potential, it can surprise everyone — including the employees themselves.

Consider the example of Maria, a supervisor in a municipal call center. When she took over, call wait times consistently exceeded the target, and staff morale was low. Instead of punishing employees for slow handling, Maria introduced growth-oriented accountability. She scheduled weekly coaching sessions where staff reviewed difficult calls and brainstormed strategies. She created a peer-mentoring system to enable experienced employees to guide newer ones. Moreover, she celebrated even the most minor incremental improvements. Within six months, average wait times had decreased by 18 percent, and employee engagement scores had risen. Maria's staff not only complied with standards, but they also developed into professionals who took ownership of their performance.

"Accountability with a growth mindset is not about catching people failing; it is about helping people grow strong enough to succeed." — Dr. Patrick C. Patrong

The lesson is clear: growth and accountability are not opposites. In fact, accountability without growth is shallow, while accountability with growth is transformative. Supervisors who see themselves as coaches rather than judges create environments where people not only meet standards but exceed them.

Section 3 — Barriers to an Accountability Mindset

If accountability is so powerful when practiced with stewardship and growth in mind, why do so many supervisors struggle to embrace it? The answer lies in the barriers — the deeply ingrained fears, habits, and external pressures that distort the understanding and application of accountability. By naming these barriers and addressing them directly, supervisors can begin to remove the obstacles that prevent accountability from becoming a constructive force.

Fear of Conflict.

Many supervisors avoid accountability conversations because they anticipate conflict. No one enjoys being accused of failure, and supervisors often fear that raising performance concerns will provoke defensiveness, hostility, or even formal grievances. This fear leads to avoidance. Deadlines slip, standards erode, and minor problems become chronic. However, the longer the issues remain unaddressed, the greater the eventual conflict will be. Courageous supervisors reframe these conversations as opportunities for growth rather than battles to be won. They enter them prepared, empathetic, and focused on solutions rather than fault.

Past Negative Experiences.

Supervisors are shaped by their own experiences of being managed. If accountability in their career has always meant punishment, micromanagement, or public shaming, they may assume that is the only model available. This "scar tissue" distorts their mindset, making them cautious or cynical. To break free, supervisors must consciously reject the negative examples they have seen and commit to building new experiences for their teams — experiences where accountability is fair, consistent, and tied to learning.

Ambiguity of Standards.

Nothing undermines accountability faster than unclear expectations. If employees are unsure what "success" looks like, holding them accountable may feel arbitrary and unfair. Supervisors then hesitate to enforce standards, fearing they will be accused of favoritism or inconsistency. Ambiguity is a leadership failure, not an employee failure. Clear standards are the foundation of accountability. Supervisors must articulate expectations in measurable and observable terms, and repeat them consistently until they become embedded in daily practice.

Political and Union Pressures.

Public-sector supervisors face unique challenges. Elected officials may demand visible results on short timelines, regardless of operational realities. Union contracts may define strict boundaries for discipline, making accountability conversations feel like walking a tightrope. Media scrutiny can magnify small mistakes into public controversies. These pressures can tempt supervisors to retreat into survival mode — doing just enough to avoid headlines or grievances.

Nevertheless, survival mode erodes leadership credibility. The better path is to lean into transparency and fairness. When supervisors clearly document expectations, provide support, and communicate decisions openly, they are better protected against political or union pushback. Accountability, when rooted in fairness, is defensible.

Cultural Inertia.

In many organizations, the status quo itself is a barrier. "This is how we have always done it" becomes the refrain. Employees and supervisors alike may resist new approaches because they fear change or because mediocrity feels safer than the risk of improvement. Breaking cultural inertia requires persistence and symbolic action. Supervisors must not only set new standards but also model them publicly. They must celebrate early adopters and demonstrate that accountability brings recognition as well as responsibility.

Magic with a Message: One illusion I sometimes perform involves restoring a torn piece of paper. The audience sees the paper ripped apart and assumes it is ruined. Nevertheless, slowly, piece by piece, it is made whole again. This performance illustrates a truth about barriers: they are not permanent. Even if accountability has been torn apart by past abuse or fear, it can be restored when leaders are willing to change their mindset and rebuild trust.

The bottom line is that barriers are not excuses. They are realities that must be acknowledged, confronted, and overcome. Supervisors who recognize these barriers in themselves and in their organizations are better equipped to lead change. The difference between those who perpetuate broken models of accountability and those who transform them lies in the willingness to face these barriers with honesty and courage.

Section 4 — Public Sector Case Snapshot: The City Inspector's Dilemma

Marcus was a city building inspector supervisor overseeing a team responsible for code enforcement. Citizens frequently complained that inspections were inconsistent, and political leaders pressured the department to "clean up the process."

Marcus's initial instinct was to blame his staff. "They are not thorough enough," he muttered. However, after reflecting on his accountability mindset, he realized the real issue was his own approach. He had not provided clear standards. Each inspector was interpreting the code differently, leading to inconsistent results.

Marcus gathered the team and reframed the issue. "I have not been clear enough about expectations," he admitted. "I take responsibility for that. Going forward, I will provide detailed checklists, and we will calibrate inspections together."

By shifting from blame to responsibility, Marcus transformed the culture. Complaints dropped as inspections became more consistent. The team felt supported rather than attacked. Political leaders took note of the improvement and praised the department. Marcus's shift in mindset reshaped not just results but also relationships.

Section 5 — Applied Tool: The Accountability Mindset Assessment

Supervisors often want to change their culture, but they are unsure of where to start. The truth is, accountability begins inside the leader. Before expecting your team to take on responsibility, you must first evaluate and strengthen your own mindset. The Accountability Mindset Assessment is designed to help you do exactly that.

This tool is not a performance evaluation for employees — it is a self-diagnostic instrument for supervisors. Its purpose is to highlight blind spots, challenge assumptions, and encourage intentional growth. The assessment comprises five key dimensions of an accountability mindset. Each dimension reflects a belief that either strengthens or weakens accountability.

Step 1 — Rate Yourself Honestly

On a scale of 1 (rarely) to 5 (consistently), rate how true each statement is of your current leadership practice:

1. **Ownership:** I take responsibility for the conditions that shape my team's performance, not just the outcomes.

2. **Developmental Approach:** I view accountability as a developmental, rather than punitive, approach.

3. **Coaching Orientation:** I use accountability conversations to coach, not condemn.

4. **Clarity:** I consistently clarify expectations and avoid ambiguity.

5. **Learning Focus:** I treat mistakes as opportunities to strengthen the system, not just evidence of failure.

Add up your scores for a total between 5 and 25.

Step 2 — Interpret Your Score

- **5–10: Blame-based mindset.** Your team likely experiences accountability as a form of punishment. Urgent change is needed to prevent disengagement.

- **11–15: Reactive mindset.** You occasionally practice

stewardship, but old habits of blame persist. Focus on clarifying expectations and responding to mistakes with curiosity and understanding.

- **16–20: Growth-developing mindset.** You are on the path to proactive accountability. Continue building systems that reinforce your developmental approach.

- **21–25: Stewardship mindset.** You consistently model ownership and growth. Your next step is to mentor other supervisors in adopting the same mindset.

Step 3 — Identify Blind Spots

Most supervisors find that at least one dimension scores lower than the others. That score reveals your blind spot — the place where your mindset needs the most attention. Write it down. For example, you may score high on Ownership and Clarity but low on Coaching Orientation. That indicates you know how to set expectations but struggle to turn accountability conversations into coaching opportunities.

Step 4 — Create a Personal Action Plan

For each blind spot, list one action you will take this month to strengthen it. Small, consistent actions are better than grand but unsustainable gestures.

- If your blind spot is **Ownership**, ask your team directly: "What conditions make it harder for you to succeed, and what can I do to change them?"

- If your blind spot is **Developmental Approach**, practice replacing phrases like "Why did you mess this up?" with "What support would help you succeed next time?"

- If your blind spot is **Coaching Orientation**, schedule brief check-ins focused not on tasks but on growth.

- If your blind spot is **Clarity**, rewrite one of your team's goals to make it more specific, measurable, and observable.

- If your blind spot is **Learning Focus**, conduct a quick "after-action review" after a project, focusing on what was learned rather than who made the error.

Worked Example 1 — Marcus, the City Inspector

Marcus scored low on Ownership. He realized he had been blaming his inspectors without providing consistent standards. His action step was to create a checklist and hold weekly calibration sessions. Within months, he saw both morale and performance improve. His blind spot became a strength through intentional action.

Worked Example 2 — Sandra, the Parks Supervisor

Sandra managed a team of groundskeepers in a municipal park system. Her assessment revealed a blind spot in Clarity. She often gave general directions, such as "Make sure the park looks good for the weekend," which left staff uncertain about priorities. After completing the assessment, Sandra rewrote her instructions into measurable standards: "Mow the north field by Thursday; empty all trash bins daily; and check playground equipment weekly for safety issues." The result was not only improved park conditions but also less stress on employees, who no longer had to guess what "looking good" meant.

Worked Example 3 — Devon, the Social Services Manager

Devon scored low on Learning Focus. Whenever a case worker made a mistake, his instinct was to issue a warning. After reflecting, he tried a different approach. He began holding monthly case reviews where staff discussed both successes and mistakes openly, with the goal of collective learning. Over time, staff morale improved, turnover decreased, and case handling became more consistent. Devon's shift from punishment to learning changed the entire department's trajectory.

Step 5 — Revisit Regularly

The Accountability Mindset Assessment is not a one-time exercise. Mindsets can slip under pressure, especially in politically sensitive or resource-constrained environments. Revisit the assessment every quarter. Compare scores over time. Celebrate progress and recommit to areas that still require growth.

The assessment can also be used in supervisor training cohorts. When supervisors discuss their scores together, they realize they are not alone in their struggles. Shared vulnerability fosters a supportive culture where accountability is understood as a means of development rather than judgment.

Section 6 — Reflection Questions

Reflection is where information becomes transformation. These questions are designed to help supervisors pause, examine their current mindset, and commit to small but meaningful changes. Take time to write down your answers or discuss them with peers. The value is not in rushing through them but in allowing them to challenge your thinking.

1. When I hear the word "accountability," what feelings arise in me — fear, confidence, blame, or stewardship? Why?

Our immediate emotional reaction often reveals the stories we carry from past experiences. If accountability makes you nervous, consider where that nervousness comes from — perhaps a past leader who used it harshly. If it makes you confident, reflect on how you have seen it practiced well. The key is to name your reaction honestly and then decide if that reaction supports or undermines the leader you want to be.

2. How have my past experiences shaped my current mindset about accountability?

Every supervisor is a product of their history. Maybe you had a boss who believed accountability meant constant surveillance, or maybe you once worked in a culture where mistakes were fatal to careers.

Those experiences leave marks. Identifying them allows you to separate what you inherited from what you choose to create. How much of your current practice is genuinely yours, and how much is simply a copy of what you endured?

3. In what ways do I unintentionally model blame rather than responsibility?

This question is uncomfortable but necessary. Think of recent conversations with your team. Did your words sound like accusations ("Why didn't you...?") or invitations ("What can we do differently?")? Did your body language communicate openness or judgment? Supervisors often communicate blame without realizing it, and subtle shifts in tone can significantly impact how accountability is received.

4. Which barriers to accountability do I most need to overcome — fear of conflict, negative past experiences, ambiguity, political pressures, or cultural inertia?

Choose one. Write it down. Then outline a specific strategy for addressing it. For example, if your barrier is a fear of conflict, commit to scripting your following accountability conversation in advance so you enter it with confidence. If it is ambiguous, draft one expectation this week in clear, measurable language. Tackling one barrier at a time is more effective than trying to conquer them all at once.

5. What practical step will I take this week to model a growth-oriented accountability mindset to my team?

The best reflections end with action. Maybe you will start by reframing one accountability conversation into a coaching moment. Maybe you will share with your team that you are committed to treating mistakes as learning opportunities. Perhaps you could introduce a five-minute" lessons learned" exercise at the end of your next staff meeting. Accountability becomes a culture when it is modeled consistently.

How would I like my team to describe me in terms of accountability?

Imagine overhearing your employees talk about you. Would they say you are fair, consistent, and supportive? Or would they say you are harsh, unpredictable, or absent? Write down three words you hope your team would use. Then ask yourself: are your current actions aligned with those words? If not, what must change?

7. How will I keep myself accountable for maintaining a healthy mindset?

Leaders also need accountability. Who in your circle can remind you when you slip back into blame or avoidance? How will you check your mindset when stress is high? Perhaps it is through journaling, peer support, or revisiting the Accountability Mindset Assessment on a quarterly basis. Without a plan, even the best intentions fade.

These questions are not an exam — there are no right or wrong answers. They are invitations to more profound honesty. Supervisors who engage with them thoughtfully will begin to notice a shift: accountability stops feeling like a burden and starts functioning as a compass, pointing them and their teams toward growth and trust.

Leadership-Centered Closing Summary

Accountability does not begin with policies, checklists, or performance reviews. It begins in the supervisor's mind. The way you think about accountability determines the way your team experiences it. A blame-based mindset produces fear and avoidance. A responsibility-based mindset produces trust and problem-solving. A growth-oriented mindset produces resilience and innovation.

This chapter has shown that supervisors must first confront their own assumptions. Are you clinging to past models of punishment, or are you willing to adopt a stewardship approach? Are you avoiding accountability conversations out of fear, or are you practicing them with fairness and courage? Are you treating mistakes as evidence of failure, or are you leveraging them as fuel for learning? The answers to these questions shape your effectiveness and the culture of your team.

The public sector is a proving ground for accountability. Citizens demand transparency, unions and political leaders apply pressure, and employees often operate under constrained resources. In such environments, supervisors who embrace a positive accountability mindset become anchors of stability. They model integrity, fairness, and courage. They create climates where employees feel safe enough to take ownership and strong enough to deliver results.

Accountability also requires persistence. Mindset is not something you adjust once and forget. It must be cultivated daily, especially when stress is high or the political landscape shifts. Supervisors who revisit their mindset, who reflect on their blind spots, and who recommit to stewardship demonstrate the discipline of leadership. Over time, they build cultures that outlast administrations and withstand public scrutiny.

"A supervisor's mindset is the soil from which accountability grows. If the soil is toxic, nothing thrives. If the soil is rich with responsibility, growth is inevitable."
— *Dr. Patrick C. Patrong*

As you close this chapter, remember that accountability is not a burden you impose after failure. It is a mindset you carry before the challenge. By shifting from blame to responsibility and adopting a growth orientation, you will not only strengthen your leadership but also elevate the people and programs entrusted to you. This is the essence of embracing accountability — not as a shadow of fear, but as a source of light and strength for everyone you lead.

SETTING CLEAR EXPECTATIONS

"Clarity is kindness. When supervisors define success clearly, they free their teams from guessing games and give them the courage to perform."

— *Dr. Patrick C. Patrong*

Introduction — The Compass of Clarity

Supervisors often underestimate the amount of energy employees expend trying to interpret unclear instructions. Ambiguous goals, vague deadlines, and shifting standards not only frustrate staff but also undermine accountability. How can employees take ownership of outcomes when they are unsure what those outcomes actually are?

Clarity is the compass of accountability. Without it, teams wander in circles. With it, they move in alignment toward shared goals. Clear expectations transform accountability from a guessing game into a fair and transparent process. They create the conditions where employees know what is required, supervisors can measure progress objectively, and organizations can deliver results consistently.

Magic with a Message: I often demonstrate this point using the "blindfold navigation" activity. A volunteer is blindfolded and asked to walk toward an object across the room. If given vague directions like "go that way," the volunteer stumbles and veers off course. However, when provided with precise guidance — such as "take three steps forward, then turn slightly left" — they succeed. The lesson is obvious: clarity transforms struggle into achievement.

This chapter explores how supervisors can set clear expectations in practice. We will examine the power of clarity, the process of defining performance standards, the importance of setting measurable goals, and strategies for effectively communicating expectations. We will examine a detailed public-sector case snapshot where unclear expectations led to problems until supervisors clarified the standard. Finally, we will introduce a practical framework and reflection prompts to ensure clarity becomes a daily leadership habit.

Section 1 — The Power of Clarity

Clarity is one of the simplest leadership practices to describe, but one of the hardest to deliver consistently. Too often, supervisors assume they have been clear when, in reality, employees are left guessing. A directive like "get this done quickly" may sound specific in the supervisor's head, but to one employee, "quickly" means by the end of the day, while to another it means sometime this week. The result is inconsistency, disappointment, and unnecessary frustration.

In public-sector organizations, where accountability is heightened by taxpayer expectations, council oversight, and constant media attention, the cost of unclear instructions is magnified. A vague memo can ripple into wasted resources, delayed services, and damaged public trust. Supervisors who fail to set clear expectations often find themselves trapped in cycles of rework, defensiveness, and blame.

The power of clarity lies in its fairness. When employees know what is expected of them, they can align their efforts, creativity, and focus toward the proper outcomes. Clarity eliminates guesswork, reduces stress, and builds trust because everyone understands the target. It also provides a solid foundation for accountability. Supervisors can only hold people fairly accountable to standards that have been defined and communicated. Without clarity, accountability collapses into arbitrariness.

Clarity also fuels efficiency. When expectations are specific, measurable, and visible, employees waste less time checking assumptions. Meetings become shorter, handoffs smoother, and progress easier to track. In an era when public-sector leaders are asked to "do more with less," clarity is not just a courtesy — it is a critical resource.

"Clarity is not control. Clarity is freedom. It frees people from confusion so they can focus on contribution."

— *Dr. Patrick C. Patrong*

Section 2 — Defining Clear Performance Standards

Clear expectations begin with clear standards. Standards answer the question: "What does good performance look like here?" Without standards, employees rely on personal judgment, which varies widely. Supervisors who avoid defining standards may think they are being flexible, but in reality, they are setting their teams up for inconsistency and conflict.

Defining standards means identifying the specific behaviors, outputs, or results that constitute success. For example, in a city sanitation department, a vague expectation might be "keep the streets clean." A clear standard, by contrast, would specify: "Trash receptacles emptied daily by 10:00 a.m.; streets swept twice weekly; graffiti removed within 48 hours of report." The difference is not just semantic — it is operational. Standards transform intentions into actions that can be observed, measured, and repeated.

Supervisors must also distinguish between **minimum standards** and **excellence standards**. Minimum standards define the baseline below which performance is unacceptable. Excellence standards motivate employees to strive for higher levels of achievement. Both are important. Minimums protect organizational credibility, while excellence goals encourage innovation and pride. When employees understand both, they know where the floor is and where the ceiling can be.

Defining standards requires engagement, not just edicts. Supervisors who involve employees in shaping standards build ownership and buy-in. Asking questions like "What would quality look like to our citizens?" or "How can we measure success fairly?" turns standard-setting into a collaborative exercise. The resulting standards are not only more transparent but also more credible because they were created in collaboration with employees.

Finally, standards must be documented. Verbal expectations fade; written standards endure. Posting standards in team spaces, embedding them in policy documents, or incorporating them into onboarding materials ensures consistency across time and personnel changes. This point is especially critical in state and municipal agencies, where leadership turnover is a common occurrence.

Section 3 — Establishing Measurable Goals and Objectives

Once standards are defined, supervisors must translate them into goals and objectives. Goals provide direction; objectives provide milestones along the way. Together, they make accountability possible. Without measurable goals, accountability becomes subjective and prone to bias.

Supervisors should embrace the SMART framework — goals that are Specific, Measurable, Achievable, Relevant, and Time-bound. For example, instead of setting the goal "improve community engagement," a SMART version would be: "Increase attendance at quarterly neighborhood meetings by 15% within the next fiscal year." This clarity transforms an aspiration into an actionable target.

In public sector environments, measurable goals carry particular weight. Citizens and elected officials want evidence that programs are working. A parks department might set a goal to "increase park usage." Nevertheless, unless it specifies "raise average weekend park attendance from 500 to 750 visitors within six months," there is no way to demonstrate progress. Specific goals provide both direction for employees and proof for stakeholders.

Supervisors must also consider cascading goals. An agency-wide objective, such as "improve citizen satisfaction by 10%," must be broken down into unit-level goals and then into individual objectives. For instance, in a DMV office, the overarching goal might cascade into a unit goal to reduce the average wait time by 15 minutes, which in turn cascades into an individual objective for clerks to process applications within a 12-minute window. This alignment ensures that every employee understands how their work contributes to the broader success of the organization.

Setting measurable goals also supports fairness in performance evaluation. Employees cannot be held accountable for vague ideals like "be a team player" or "show initiative." Nevertheless, they can be evaluated on whether they completed 95% of assigned cases within deadlines or whether they accurately documented 100% of safety checks. Measurable objectives protect both employees and supervisors by creating transparency.

"Expectations without measurement are like directions without a map. Everyone may start walking, but no one knows if they are headed the right way."
— *Dr. Patrick C. Patrong*

Section 4 — Communicating Expectations Effectively

Even the clearest standards and goals are useless if they are not communicated effectively. Too often, supervisors assume that once something has been said once, it has been understood. In reality, people interpret instructions differently, and messages compete with dozens of other demands in the workplace. Effective communication requires intentionality, repetition, and feedback.

First, supervisors must **use plain language**. Bureaucratic jargon or overly technical terms confuse employees and obscure expectations. "Ensure compliance with applicable protocols" is vague; "Complete the daily safety checklist before operating equipment" is clear and concise. The goal is not to sound impressive but to be understood.

Second, expectations must be **repeated consistently**. Clarity fades if it is not reinforced. Embedding expectations into weekly briefings, written materials, and performance reviews ensures they remain visible. Repetition should not feel like nagging but like alignment. Athletes practice the fundamentals daily, not because they are slow learners but because excellence requires reinforcement.

Third, communication must be **two-way**. Supervisors should not just announce expectations but check for understanding. Asking employees to restate the goal in their own words reveals whether clarity has been achieved. Questions such as "What does success look like for you on this task?" or "What might get in the way of meeting this goal?" uncover assumptions and surface potential obstacles early.

Finally, supervisors must **model the expectations themselves**. If punctuality is expected, the supervisor should arrive on time. If reports must be concise, the supervisor's reports should set the standard. Nothing undermines communication faster than hypocrisy.

"Expectations are not clear until they are both spoken and seen. A leader's actions are the loudest form of communication."

— Dr. Patrick C. Patrong

Section 5 — Public Sector Case Snapshot: The Transit Scheduling Confusion

Scene 1 — The Problem Emerges

Tasha supervised a scheduling unit in the city's transit authority. Riders frequently complained that buses were late or overcrowded. Operators said schedules were unrealistic, while managers insisted they had provided clear directives. The truth was that expectations had been poorly communicated.

Scene 2 — Vague Directives

Supervisors had told operators to "maintain on-time service," but they had never defined what "on-time" meant. Some operators considered arriving within five minutes of the scheduled time acceptable, while others considered 10 minutes acceptable. A few believed avoiding early arrivals mattered more than avoiding late ones. Passengers, meanwhile, expected buses to arrive exactly when posted. The mismatch created frustration for everyone.

Scene 3 — Resetting Expectations

Tasha realized the problem was not a lack of effort but a lack of clarity. She convened a meeting with operators and said, "I take responsibility for not defining expectations precisely. From today forward, 'on-time' means arriving no more than three minutes early and no more than five minutes late. Anything outside that window is considered off-schedule." She posted the standard in break rooms, added it to the handbook, and reinforced it in weekly updates.

Scene 4 — Communicating for Understanding

Tasha did not stop at announcements. She asked operators to describe the expectation in their own words and to share scenarios where meeting it might be difficult. One driver explained that construction on his route made the standard unrealistic. Tasha worked with him to adjust his schedule. This situation reinforced that accountability was not about punishment, but about setting people up to succeed.

Scene 5 — The Outcome

Within six months, on-time performance improved by 22 percent, passenger complaints declined, and operators reported greater confidence in knowing what was expected. Councilmembers praised the progress publicly, citing it as evidence of improved accountability in city services. The transformation began not with stricter enforcement but with more transparent communication.

Section 6 — Applied Tool: The Expectations Framework

Supervisors can use a simple three-step framework to ensure

expectations are set clearly and communicated effectively. The framework is called **ACE** — Articulate, Confirm, Embed.

Step 1 — Articulate Expectations Clearly

State what success looks like in specific, measurable, observable terms. Avoid jargon and vagueness.

Example: Instead of "Keep the facility safe," say "Conduct daily safety checks using the standard checklist and report any hazards immediately."

Step 2 — Confirm Understanding

Do not assume clarity. Ask employees to restate expectations in their own words. Explore possible challenges.

Example: "Tell me how you would explain this safety standard to a new hire. What obstacles might keep you from meeting it?"

Step 3 — Embed Expectations in Practice

Integrate expectations into regular routines. Post them visibly, reference them in meetings, and reinforce them in evaluations.

Example: Include the safety checklist in shift change briefings, add it to performance reviews, and post it in the break room.

Worked Example 1 — Public Works

A public works supervisor told staff to "improve snow removal efficiency." That directive was too vague. Using ACE, he rephrased:

Articulate: "Clear priority roads within six hours of snowfall ending."

- **Confirm:** Staff repeated the timeline and identified potential challenges, such as equipment shortages.

- **Embed:** The standard was posted in work bays, reviewed in winter briefings, and added to shift logs.

Worked Example 2 — Human Services

A supervisor in a child protective services office instructed caseworkers to "respond to urgent cases quickly." The phrase "quickly" had different meanings for different workers. She applied ACE:

- **Articulate:** "All urgent cases must be contacted within two hours of assignment."

- **Confirm:** Each worker explained how they would meet the requirement and flagged times when the workload might make it difficult.

- **Embed:** The two-hour standard was added to the case management system, included in orientation, and reinforced in weekly meetings.

Worked Example 3 — Parks and Recreation

Staff were instructed to "keep playgrounds in good shape," which resulted in uneven maintenance. The supervisor clarified through ACE:

- **Articulate:** "Inspect each playground weekly, complete the inspection form, and address any hazard within 24 hours."

- **Confirm:** Staff members walked through the inspection form during training to ensure understanding.

- **Embed:** Completed forms were filed electronically, and inspections were logged for public transparency.

"Clear expectations are the foundation of fair accountability. Without clarity, supervisors judge. With clarity, supervisors lead."

— Dr. Patrick C. Patrong

Section 7 — Reflection Questions

Reflection transforms clarity from theory into practice. These questions are designed to help supervisors examine their current habits, identify areas for improvement, and commit to enhancing how they set and communicate expectations.

1. How clear are my current expectations?

Think about the last primary directive you gave your team. If I asked three employees to explain it, would their answers match? If not, what does that reveal about your communication?

2. Do I rely too heavily on verbal instructions?

Verbal communication fades quickly. What systems do I have in place to ensure expectations are documented and visible? How can I improve my consistency in writing things down?

3. How do I define "success" for my team?

Is success measured by vague impressions ("doing a good job") or by specific outcomes tied to organizational goals? Write one concrete measure you could introduce this week.

4. Have unclear expectations caused frustration on my team?

Recall a moment when staff seemed confused, overwhelmed, or disengaged. What role did unclear direction play? How could clarity have changed the outcome?

5. How do I check for understanding after giving instructions?

Do I ask employees to repeat back expectations? Do I invite questions about barriers? If not, what practice can I add to ensure genuine comprehension?

6. Do my standards include both minimums and excellence goals?

Think about a current project. Have I defined the minimum acceptable standard and also challenged the team to strive for excellence? If not, what statement could I add to clarify both?

7. How can I model the expectations I set?

Reflect on whether your own actions reinforce or contradict your stated standards. Choose one expectation you will personally demonstrate more consistently this week.

Leadership-Centered Closing Summary

Accountability without clarity is chaos. Supervisors who fail to define and communicate expectations set their teams up for confusion, inconsistency, and frustration. Supervisors who embrace clarity, on the other hand, create fairness, trust, and alignment.

In this chapter, we examined how clear standards and measurable goals form the foundation for accountability. We explored the importance of communicating expectations effectively, not just announcing them but confirming and embedding them. We examined how one supervisor in a transit authority transitioned from vague directives to precise standards, resulting in improved outcomes and restored public trust. We introduced the ACE framework — Articulate, Confirm, Embed — to provide supervisors with a practical roadmap for setting clear and effective expectations.

The lesson is simple but profound: clarity is kindness. When supervisors are clear, employees feel respected because they are no longer forced to guess or interpret shifting signals. Clarity also protects supervisors, because it creates a fair basis for accountability. No one can say "I did not know" when expectations are documented, confirmed, and reinforced.

"Supervisors who set clear standards build trust twice — once by defining what matters, and again by holding everyone to it fairly."

— *Dr. Patrick C. Patrong*

As you step forward, commit to making clarity a habit in your leadership. Write it down. Say it aloud. Check for understanding. Embed it in practice. When your team knows exactly what success looks like, they are far more likely to achieve it. Furthermore, when accountability is built on clarity, it becomes not a source of fear but a platform for fairness, growth, and results.

COMMUNICATION FOR ACCOUNTABILITY

"Accountability travels on the road of communication. If the road is blocked, accountability never arrives."

— Dr. Patrick C. Patrong

Introduction — Words That Build or Break Accountability

Communication is the lifeblood of accountability. Standards, expectations, and commitments mean nothing if they are not communicated clearly, consistently, and credibly. In fact, most accountability failures are not failures of effort or intent — they are failures of communication. A supervisor may think they set clear goals, but if employees interpret the message differently, frustration and misalignment follow.

For supervisors in state and municipal organizations, communication carries even greater weight. Citizens, council members, auditors, and union representatives all scrutinize how messages are conveyed. A poorly worded directive can spiral into grievance claims. A confusing memo can delay service delivery for thousands. A careless comment at a public meeting can undermine community trust. Communication is not just an internal management tool — it is a leadership responsibility with public consequences.

Magic with a Message: In workshops, I sometimes perform the "newspaper water" illusion. I pour water into a rolled-up newspaper. Everyone expects it to leak or disintegrate. Instead, the paper holds, and the water disappears. The trick shows this truth: appearances can deceive. Just because words are spoken does not mean they have landed. Just because an email is sent does not mean it has been read or understood. Supervisors must go beyond appearances to ensure communication has truly delivered clarity.

In this chapter, we will explore communication strategies that promote accountability. We will examine techniques for delivering constructive feedback, methods for addressing performance gaps, and the critical role of active listening. We will also analyze a detailed public-sector case snapshot where poor communication undermined results until a supervisor changed the approach. Finally, we will introduce a practical tool that supervisors can apply immediately to strengthen accountability through communication.

Section 1 — Communication as the Engine of Accountability

Accountability cannot exist in silence. Even the clearest standards and the strongest intentions require communication to bridge the gap between what leaders want and what employees understand. Communication is the engine that moves accountability from concept to practice. Without it, supervisors are left to guess about performance, and employees are left to guess about expectations.

In many organizations, accountability fails not because people lack the necessary skills or motivation, but because messages are lost in translation. A supervisor thinks they have explained priorities, but the team interprets them differently. An email intended to clarify policy is buried under dozens of other messages. A public announcement emphasizes urgency but omits detail, leaving employees scrambling to fill in the gaps. The result is confusion that feels like incompetence, when in reality it is poor communication.

Supervisors must approach communication as a discipline, not an afterthought. Clear accountability communication has three key characteristics: it is specific, timely, and **two-way**. Specificity ensures that employees know exactly what is required of them. Timeliness ensures that guidance arrives when it is needed, not after the fact. Two-way communication ensures that understanding is confirmed rather than assumed.

For public-sector supervisors, the stakes are high. Communication errors can quickly become public failures. A misplaced phrase in a council presentation can fuel headlines. An ambiguous directive to frontline staff can lead to uneven service delivery, which can anger citizens. A vague policy memo can open the door to grievances. When accountability rests on communication, clarity is not just a management tactic — it is a public trust requirement.

Section 2 — Providing Constructive Feedback

Feedback is one of the most potent forms of accountability communication. Done well, it helps employees grow, strengthens performance, and reinforces trust. Done poorly, it can damage morale, create resentment, and undermine credibility.

Constructive feedback has three essential qualities: it is **specific**, balanced, and **actionable**.

Specificity prevents defensiveness. Instead of saying "You are not reliable," a supervisor might say, "You missed three report deadlines this month." Facts are more complicated to dispute than vague judgments.

Balance ensures that employees hear both strengths and areas for improvement. Too much focus on weaknesses discourages. Too much emphasis on strengths without correction enables mediocrity. Constructive feedback acknowledges what is working while clearly pointing out what needs improvement.

Actionability transforms feedback from criticism into coaching. Instead of saying, "Your reports are sloppy," the supervisor might say, "Your analysis is strong, but several charts were missing labels. Let us review the template together so the next report is clear." The employee leaves not only corrected but also equipped to do better.

Magic with a Message: In my training sessions, I sometimes use the "sponge ball" illusion — two sponge balls placed in the hand appear to multiply. Feedback works the same way: when given constructively, it has a multiplying impact. A single conversation can have a ripple effect, influencing many actions and improving performance long after the meeting ends.

Supervisors should also pay attention to tone and setting. Public criticism embarrasses employees and often creates resistance. Private, respectful conversations foster openness. Timing matters too — feedback delivered weeks after an incident loses impact. The best practice is to provide feedback promptly after the event, while emotions are still fresh and details are still fresh in memory.

In the public sector, constructive feedback must also navigate union rules and formal processes. Documentation may be required, and language must be professional. Nevertheless, these constraints do not prevent constructive dialogue; they simply require supervisors to be thoughtful and precise in their approach. In fact, well-documented constructive feedback often strengthens the supervisor's position because it shows fairness and due process.

Section 3 — Addressing Performance Gaps

Performance gaps are the places where accountability feels most uncomfortable. It is easy to praise success and harder to confront failure. However, supervisors who avoid addressing gaps erode credibility with both employees and stakeholders. Accountability requires confronting gaps directly, fairly, and constructively.

The first step in addressing a performance gap is to **diagnose the cause**. Gaps can arise from three sources: a lack of skill, a lack of will, or a lack of clarity. If an employee lacks a skill, the solution is typically training or coaching. If the employee lacks motivation, the solution may involve providing recognition or, in some cases, disciplinary processes.

If the employee lacks clarity, the solution is communication. Supervisors who skip diagnosis risk applying the wrong remedy.

The second step is to **have the conversation early**. Waiting until frustration boils over makes the discussion harder. A timely, direct conversation prevents minor problems from becoming entrenched habits. Early conversations also signal fairness — the supervisor cares enough to intervene before failure becomes irreversible.

The third step is to **frame the gap in terms of outcomes, not personal flaws**. Instead of "You are careless," a supervisor might say, "The incomplete data in last week's report delayed our ability to present accurate information to the council." This version shifts the focus from personality to performance, from judgment to problem-solving.

Supervisors should also use the opportunity to **invite the employee into problem-solving**. Asking "What support do you need to close this gap?" empowers employees to take ownership of the solution. Accountability is not imposed; it is co-created.

Public Sector Example: A county clerk repeatedly submitted late filings, frustrating colleagues and external stakeholders. Instead of accusing the clerk of laziness, the supervisor asked diagnostic questions to determine the cause of the issue. They discovered that the clerk was juggling conflicting deadlines from multiple departments. Together, they redesigned the workflow and set up a shared calendar. The filings were completed on time, and morale improved. The gap was not a case of willful neglect, but rather a systems issue revealed through conversation.

"Addressing gaps is not about exposing weakness. It is about closing the distance between potential and performance."

— *Dr. Patrick C. Patrong*

Section 4 — Active Listening and Open Dialogue

Accountability is not a monologue delivered by the supervisor. It is a dialogue dependent on listening as much as speaking. When supervisors practice active listening, they send a powerful signal: "I value your perspective, even when performance must improve." This simple shift builds trust and makes employees more willing to accept responsibility.

Active listening requires more than nodding politely. It involves giving full attention, reflecting what is heard, and asking clarifying questions. Instead of rushing to judgment, supervisors pause to gain a deeper understanding. For example, if an employee consistently misses deadlines, the supervisor who listens actively may discover employees are overloaded with conflicting tasks or unclear instructions cause delays. Listening changes the supervisor's response from blame to collaboration.

Open dialogue goes hand in hand with listening. Supervisors must create spaces where employees feel safe to raise concerns, admit mistakes, and share ideas. This discussion requires not only open-door policies but also consistent behaviors. If employees who speak up are punished or dismissed, dialogue dies quickly. However, if their input is acknowledged and acted upon, dialogue flourishes.

Magic with a Message: I sometimes use the "bill in the orange" trick. An audience member's signed bill vanishes and reappears inside an orange. The point is that what goes in must be retrieved with care. Similarly, what employees share in dialogue must be handled responsibly. If supervisors ignore or misuse what they hear, trust is lost. Nevertheless, when they handle it with care, accountability deepens.

Active listening and open dialogue are not soft skills; they are accountability tools. They ensure that supervisors respond to real issues rather than assumptions, and they build the credibility that makes accountability sustainable.

Section 5 — Public Sector Case Snapshot: The Housing Department Breakdown

Scene 1 — Confusion on the Front Line

The city's housing department was responsible for processing rental assistance applications. Demand was high, and delays were common.

Citizens complained to councilmembers, who accused the department of inefficiency. Staff morale plummeted. At the center of the storm was Janet, a mid-level supervisor.

Scene 2 — The Communication Problem

Janet's team had been told to "process applications as quickly as possible." Nevertheless, the directive was vague. Some staff rushed through cases, missing details that led to errors and appeals. Others took excessive time double-checking, creating bottlenecks. The result was uneven performance, angry applicants, and conflicting statistics that made the department look disorganized.

Scene 3 — Listening to Understand

Instead of tightening control, Janet chose to listen. She called a meeting and asked each staff member to describe how they interpreted "as quickly as possible." The answers varied wildly. Some thought it meant 24 hours, others thought it meant three days, while a few assumed a week was sufficient. Janet realized the failure was not a lack of effort, but a lack of clarity.

Scene 4 — Resetting Expectations with Dialogue

Janet reframed the conversation. "I take responsibility for not giving you a clear definition. Let us set one together. What is a realistic turnaround time that balances speed with accuracy?" After discussion, the team agreed on 48 hours for standard cases and five business days for complex ones. Janet documented the standard, posted it publicly, and built it into the tracking system.

Scene 5 — Results and Recognition

Within three months, turnaround times stabilized, error rates dropped by 30 percent, and citizen complaints declined. Councilmembers acknowledged the improvement, and staff reported higher morale because expectations were now transparent and fair. The lesson was simple: accountability had failed due to poor communication, and it was restored through listening and open dialogue.

Section 6 — Applied Tool: The CLEAR Communication Model

Supervisors can strengthen accountability communication by applying the **CLEAR** model: Concise, Listening-centered, Empathetic, Action-focused, Repeated.

Concise

Say what needs to be said in straightforward language. Eliminate jargon and ambiguity.

Example: Instead of "Ensure compliance with administrative protocols," say "Submit your weekly time sheet by Friday at 5 p.m."

Listening-centered

Communication is not complete until the receiver confirms they have understood. Invite employees to restate the expectation or share any concerns they may have.

Example: After explaining a new process, ask, "How would you explain this to a new hire?"

Empathetic

Acknowledge the employee's perspective. Accountability delivered without empathy feels harsh.

Example: "I understand the new software is frustrating. Let us walk through it together to complete the reports on time."

Action-focused

Always connect communication to a specific, observable action.

Example: "Call clients within 24 hours of receiving a case file" is an actionable statement. "Stay on top of your cases" is not.

Repeated

Clarity requires reinforcement. Important messages should be delivered in multiple formats — spoken, written, and modeled.

Example: Announce a safety standard in a meeting, post it in work areas, and demonstrate it during inspections.

Worked Example — Code Enforcement Unit

A supervisor told inspectors to "improve community interactions." The message was vague. Using CLEAR, she reframed:

- **Concise:** "Introduce yourself by name and badge number at every inspection."

- **Listening-centered:** She asked inspectors to role-play how they would greet residents.

- **Empathetic:** She acknowledged that some interactions would be tense, but emphasized the importance of professionalism.

- **Action-focused:** She specified, "Document resident interactions in the log immediately after inspection."

- **Repeated:** She posted the protocol, reinforced it in weekly briefings, and modeled it herself during ride-alongs.

Within six months, the number of complaint calls decreased, and citizen satisfaction rose. The change was not additional enforcement but more transparent communication.

"Accountability is carried in words. When words are clear, fair, and repeated, accountability is sustained." — Dr. Patrick C. Patrong.

Section 7 — Reflection Questions

Reflection is the bridge between information and transformation. Use these prompts for personal journaling or team discussions. Each is designed to challenge your assumptions about how you communicate accountability.

1. Do I assume clarity without checking for understanding?

Think of the last directive you gave. Did you ask employees to restate it in their own words? If not, how might their interpretation differ from yours?

2. Do I balance corrective feedback with recognition?

Review your last three feedback conversations. Were they only focused on problems, or did you also acknowledge what employees were doing well? What message are you sending about accountability?

3. When I confront performance gaps, do I diagnose the cause or jump to conclusions?

Reflect on a recent gap. Was it caused by lack of skill, lack of will, or lack of clarity? Did your response match the root cause?

4. How effective am I at listening?

Do employees feel safe bringing me problems? How often do I interrupt or move too quickly to solutions without understanding the full story? What practice could help me listen better?

5. Do I create open dialogue where employees can share barriers?

Consider whether your team meetings encourage honesty or suppress it. What ritual, question, or process could you add to make dialogue safer?

6. Do I adapt my communication for public-sector realities?

Consider how political pressures, union environments, or media scrutiny influence your communication. Do you document well? Do you choose words carefully? Where can you strengthen?

7. How will I improve accountability communication?

Pick one action — perhaps scripting your feedback in advance, using the CLEAR model for a new policy, or scheduling a listening session. Write it down, and hold yourself accountable to it.

Leadership-Centered Closing Summary

Communication is the lifeline of accountability. Without clear, consistent, and credible communication, even the best standards and goals collapse. Supervisors who master accountability communication create environments where expectations are understood, feedback is constructive, and performance gaps become opportunities for growth rather than sources of fear.

This chapter has highlighted the role of specificity, timeliness, and two-way dialogue in communication. We explored how constructive feedback reinforces growth, how addressing performance gaps requires diagnosis and fairness, and how active listening transforms accountability from a lecture into a conversation. The public-sector case snapshots reminded us that unclear communication can derail programs, while clear and empathetic dialogue can restore trust. Ultimately, the CLEAR model offered a practical framework for integrating communication practices into daily leadership.

Supervisors in the public sector cannot afford vague or careless communication. Too much is at stake — public trust, employee morale, and the credibility of institutions. When communication is disciplined, empathetic, and action-focused, accountability thrives.

"Supervisors who listen as much as they speak create teams that not only hear expectations but live them."

— Dr. Patrick C. Patrong

As you close this chapter, commit to practicing accountability communication daily. Be concise, check for understanding, show empathy, focus on action, and repeat until expectations are embedded. When communication becomes clear, accountability becomes fair. Furthermore, when accountability is fair, teams not only comply — they contribute, grow, and excel.

BUILDING A CULTURE OF ACCOUNTABILITY

"A culture of accountability is not built in a day — it is built daily."

— Dr. Patrick C. Patrong

Introduction — From Individual Acts to Collective Norms

Accountability cannot survive as a one-time event or a single conversation. To be sustainable, it must become part of the culture — the shared values, norms, and behaviors that guide how people act when no one is watching. A supervisor may set clear expectations and hold individuals responsible. However, unless accountability is woven into the daily fabric of the team, it will fade as soon as pressure shifts or leadership changes.

Culture is influential because it operates silently. Employees absorb cues about what is normal from the way supervisors respond to mistakes, the standards consistently enforced, and the stories shared in break rooms and staff meetings. If accountability is practiced fairly, consistently, and visibly, it becomes contagious. Team members begin to hold themselves and one another accountable, even when the supervisor is not present.

In the public sector, fostering a culture of accountability is particularly crucial. Supervisors often inherit teams that have been shaped by years of shifting leadership and political turnover. Employees may have learned that accountability means surviving scrutiny rather than pursuing excellence. Citizens may have grown skeptical about whether government programs deliver on promises. In this environment, supervisors must work deliberately to create a culture where accountability is not driven by fear of punishment, but by pride in responsibility.

Magic with a Message: I often use the "linking rings" illusion to demonstrate this point. Separate rings appear independent, but when linked, they form a chain that is stronger together. A culture of accountability works the same way. Individual acts of responsibility, when linked by shared norms and reinforced daily, create a chain that can withstand pressure. Alone, each act may falter; together, they create strength and resilience.

In this chapter, we will explore how supervisors can shape experiences and beliefs to build a culture of accountability, encourage teamwork and collaboration, and recognize and reward accountability in ways that sustain motivation. We will also examine a public-sector case snapshot of a department that shifted its culture from defensive avoidance to proactive ownership. Finally, we will present a practical framework that supervisors can use to assess and strengthen their teams' accountability culture.

Section 1 — Creating a Supportive and Empowering Work Environment

A culture of accountability does not begin with punishment; it begins with support. Employees cannot take responsibility for outcomes if they lack the tools, resources, or authority to perform their jobs effectively. Supervisors who expect accountability without empowerment create frustration. Those who pair high expectations with real support create energy, trust, and commitment.

Support begins with resources. A city public works crew cannot be accountable for filling potholes if they do not have adequate asphalt, functioning trucks, or safe equipment. A social services team cannot be accountable for case resolution if its caseloads are unmanageable. Supervisors must advocate upward for the resources their teams need and downward for the fair distribution of those resources. Support also includes training, mentoring, and access to information. Employees cannot take ownership of outcomes if they feel unprepared.

Empowerment goes further. It means giving employees enough authority to make decisions that affect their work. Micromanagement suffocates accountability because it signals that the supervisor does not trust the employee to take ownership of their results. Empowered employees, on the other hand, are more likely to innovate and take initiative. In the public sector, empowerment can be challenging due to the presence of regulations and protocols. Nevertheless, even within constraints, supervisors can grant decision-making power — such as authorizing field inspectors to approve minor adjustments without waiting for managerial sign-off, or enabling front-line clerks to resolve simple customer complaints on the spot.

The supervisor's role is to set the boundaries clearly and then step back. Boundaries define the scope of authority, and stepping back demonstrates trust and respect. When employees succeed, supervisors celebrate their initiative and success. When mistakes occur, supervisors treat them as learning opportunities rather than reasons to claw back authority. Over time, this balance of support and empowerment creates a culture where accountability is not feared but embraced.

"Accountability without empowerment is like demanding a harvest without planting seeds. Supervisors must invest before they expect." — Dr. Patrick C. Patrong.

Section 2 — Encouraging Teamwork and Collaboration

Accountability flourishes in teams where people see themselves as connected rather than isolated. When employees view accountability as an individual burden, they may hide mistakes or engage in destructive competition. When accountability is framed as a shared responsibility, collaboration increases and results improve.

Teamwork begins with shared goals. When a department defines success collectively — such as reducing emergency response times or enhancing citizen satisfaction — individuals see how their contributions align with a larger mission. This sense of shared purpose reduces blame-shifting and encourages problem-solving. Instead of saying "That is not my fault," employees say "How can we fix this together?"

Collaboration also requires transparency. Supervisors should establish systems that make progress visible to all, such as dashboards, team check-ins, or shared tracking documents. Transparency encourages peer accountability. When employees can see how the team is performing, they are more likely to encourage one another and less likely to cut corners.

In public-sector environments, collaboration is essential because many services span multiple departments. A city's sanitation department may rely on coordination with the transportation department for street closures, or a public health program may need cooperation from schools and nonprofits. Supervisors who encourage cross-functional teamwork build cultures where accountability is not confined to silos but spread across networks.

Practical strategies for encouraging collaboration include cross-training, peer mentoring, and joint problem-solving sessions. Supervisors can assign projects that require cooperation between employees with different strengths, ensuring that accountability becomes a collective habit. Recognition should also emphasize teamwork — celebrating not only individual achievements but also team successes.

Magic with a Message: In one exercise, I link three ropes together and then separate them again. The visual reinforces the point: accountability is stronger when individuals are tied together in shared effort. Just as the ropes can form a single cord, employees can form a united culture where responsibility is distributed, not hoarded.

"When accountability is shared, collaboration becomes the culture. Teams that succeed together are stronger than individuals who survive alone." — Dr. Patrick C. Patrong.

Section 3 — Recognizing and Rewarding Accountability

For accountability to become a cultural norm, it must be visible and celebrated. Employees are far more likely to repeat behaviors that are acknowledged and rewarded. Supervisors who notice acts of ownership — even small ones — send a message that accountability is valued, not merely demanded.

Recognition does not have to be elaborate. A sincere "thank you" in a staff meeting, a note of appreciation, or a shout-out in a weekly update can be powerful reinforcements. What matters most is timeliness and sincerity. Recognition delivered months later feels perfunctory; recognition given in the moment reinforces the connection between behavior and reward.

In public-sector organizations, where financial rewards may be limited, symbolic recognition becomes especially important. Certificates, letters from agency leaders, or opportunities to represent the team at conferences can signal value and respect. Supervisors should also create peer recognition opportunities, where employees can highlight one another's accountability. This concept builds community and multiplies the impact of praise.

Supervisors must also be careful to reward accountability behaviors, not just outcomes. If an employee takes ownership of a problem, raises it early, and works toward a solution, that behavior should be recognized even if the outcome is imperfect. By rewarding the behavior, supervisors foster a culture where accountability is consistently practiced, not just when success is guaranteed.

"When accountability is recognized, it becomes repeated. What leaders celebrate, cultures replicate." — Dr. Patrick C. Patrong.

Section 4 — Public Sector Case Snapshot: The Parks Department Transformation

Scene 1 — A Culture of Excuses

The city parks department had a reputation for poor maintenance. Citizens frequently complained about overgrown fields, broken equipment, and overflowing trash cans. Council meetings were filled with frustration. Internally, staff had adopted a culture of excuses: "We do not have enough staff," "That is not my area," or "The budget is too small." Supervisors echoed these excuses upward, deflecting responsibility. Accountability was absent.

Scene 2 — A New Supervisor Arrives

When Denise took over as supervisor, she faced skepticism. Staff assumed she would either blame them or burn out. Instead, Denise started by taking responsibility. In her first meeting, she said, "I cannot promise more staff or money, but I can promise that I will take responsibility for improving our results. We will do the best with what we have, and we will build a culture where accountability is normal."

Scene 3 — Shaping Experiences

Denise introduced new routines. Every Monday, crews walked the parks together and noted maintenance issues. On Wednesdays, they reviewed progress. On Fridays, Denise held a brief recognition session where she highlighted acts of accountability — such as the groundskeeper who stayed late to repair broken swings or the crew that reorganized tools for faster access. These rituals created consistent experiences that reinforced a sense of responsibility.

Scene 4 — Building Beliefs

At first, the staff were skeptical. Years of blame and excuses had created cynicism. However, as Denise continued to model ownership and celebrate accountability, beliefs shifted. Employees began to say, "We can fix this," rather than, "It is not my job." They noticed that Denise did not punish mistakes but treated them as learning opportunities. This response significantly reshaped the department's belief system.

Scene 5 — Results and Recognition

Within a year, citizen complaints dropped by 45 percent. Council members praised the visible improvements. Local newspapers ran a story about how the parks department had "turned the corner." More importantly, staff morale improved. Employees reported feeling proud of their work again. Accountability had become part of the culture — not because of new funding or equipment, but because a supervisor deliberately built experiences, reinforced beliefs, and celebrated responsibility.

Scene 6 — The Lesson

Denise reflected later: "We did not get more resources, but we created more results by changing our mindset. Accountability became a culture because it was modeled, supported, and rewarded." Her approach illustrates how supervisors can transform environments of avoidance into cultures of pride and ownership.

"Supervisors who consistently celebrate accountability turn excuses into excellence." — Dr. Patrick C. Patrong.

Section 5 — Applied Tool: The Culture Builder Framework

Building a culture of accountability is not a matter of guesswork. Supervisors can use a practical tool to assess and shape culture systematically. I call it the **Culture Builder Framework**, which focuses on four areas: Experiences, Beliefs, Behaviors, and Results.

Step 1 — Shape Experiences

Ask: What experiences are my team members having on a daily basis? Do meetings start with clarity or confusion? Do mistakes lead to blame or learning? Experiences form the foundation of culture. Supervisors can intentionally design experiences that reinforce accountability, such as regular after-action reviews or recognition rituals.

Step 2 — Strengthen Beliefs

Beliefs are the stories employees tell themselves. If their experience is that accountability leads to punishment, they will believe mistakes must be hidden. If their experience is that accountability leads to support, they will believe speaking up is safe. Supervisors shape beliefs by modeling responsibility, reinforcing fairness, and celebrating ownership.

Step 3 — Encourage Behaviors

Beliefs drive behaviors. Employees who believe accountability is fair are more likely to take initiative, report problems promptly, and support one another. Supervisors can encourage these behaviors by making them visible and rewarding them consistently.

Step 4 — Track Results

When experiences, beliefs, and behaviors align, results follow. Improved service delivery, higher employee morale, and stronger community trust are natural outcomes. Supervisors should document and share these results, showing the connection between culture and performance.

Worked Example 1 — Emergency Response Unit

A supervisor in a city's emergency response unit noticed that dispatchers were hesitant to admit errors in call routing. The culture punished mistakes harshly, so people hid them. Using the Culture Builder Framework, the supervisor introduced after-shift debriefs where mistakes were openly discussed without blame. Over time, dispatchers began to believe that admitting errors led to solutions, not punishment. Behaviors changed: staff reported issues sooner, and routing accuracy improved by 20 percent.

Worked Example 2 — Library Services\

The municipal library team struggled with uneven customer service. Some staff went above and beyond, while others did the minimum. The supervisor shaped experiences by launching a weekly "service story" share, where staff highlighted moments of accountability — a librarian who stayed late to help a student or a clerk who caught an error before it reached the public. These stories shaped beliefs that accountability was noticed and valued. Behaviors shifted, and customer satisfaction scores rose steadily.

"Cultures do not shift through speeches. They shift through daily experiences, reinforced beliefs, visible behaviors, and proven results."

— *Dr. Patrick C. Patrong.*

Section 6 — Reflection Questions

Use these questions to consider how you are currently shaping accountability culture in your team:

1. What daily experiences on my team reinforce accountability? What daily experiences undermine it?
   Think about meetings, recognition, and responses to mistakes.

2. What beliefs about accountability do my employees hold?
   Do they see it as punishment, fairness, or growth? How do I know?

3. What behaviors am I rewarding most often?
   Am I unintentionally rewarding excuse-making or avoidance by ignoring it?

4. How transparent are our results?
   Do employees see the connection between accountability and outcomes, or do results feel distant and disconnected from work?

5. What one ritual could I introduce this month to reinforce accountability?
   It could be a weekly recognition moment, a simple after-action review, or a shared progress dashboard.

Leadership-Centered Closing Summary

Accountability becomes sustainable only when it becomes a cultural norm. A culture of accountability emerges when supervisors deliberately shape experiences, strengthen beliefs, encourage behaviors, and track results. It grows when employees are supported, empowered, and celebrated for taking ownership. It thrives when teamwork and collaboration replace blame and avoidance.

The public-sector stories remind us that accountability cultures can be built even in environments of scarce resources and political pressure. Denise transformed her parks department not by adding budget but by changing daily habits and recognizing responsibility. Supervisors everywhere can do the same: culture is not about what you have, but about what you reinforce.

"A culture of accountability is built one conversation, one recognition, and one shared result at a time." — Dr. Patrick C. Patrong.

"Leaders who cultivate accountability daily plant seeds of trust that communities will harvest for years." — Dr. Patrick C. Patrong

As you move forward, remember that culture is contagious. The way you speak, act, and respond becomes the model your team imitates. If you want accountability to endure beyond your presence, build it into the culture — where it is practiced daily, celebrated openly, and sustained collectively.

ACCOUNTABILITY TOOLS AND SYSTEMS

"Systems strengthen accountability. Tools make responsibility visible, measurable, and sustainable."

— Dr. Patrick C. Patrong

Introduction — From Intention to Infrastructure

Accountability cannot survive on intentions alone. Even the most dedicated supervisors and committed employees need systems that make responsibility visible, measurable, and repeatable. Without tools and structures, accountability remains subjective — dependent on memory, mood, or chance. With tools and systems, accountability becomes embedded in daily practice, supported by processes that ensure fairness and transparency.

In public-sector organizations, the need for systems is especially urgent. Supervisors face high scrutiny from citizens, auditors, union representatives, and political leaders. Promises of accountability ring hollow if they are not backed by evidence. Tools and systems provide that evidence. They create the documentation, data, and consistency that protect both supervisors and employees.

Tools do not replace leadership; they reinforce it. A poorly designed system can overwhelm staff with bureaucracy and undermine morale. Nevertheless, a well-designed system enhances accountability by clarifying expectations, tracking progress, and ensuring follow-through. Supervisors must therefore be discerning. The goal is not to adopt every available tool, but to select and implement systems that support accountability without overwhelming the team with excessive bureaucracy.

Magic with a Message: In one exercise, I use the "cups and balls" illusion. A ball vanishes under one cup and reappears under another. The point is simple: without systems, accountability is like that ball — it disappears when pressure comes and reappears only when convenient. With systems, the ball stays where it belongs, visible to all.

In this chapter, we will examine the various tools and systems that promote accountability. We will examine performance measurement tools, the use of technology for tracking progress, and the development of accountability processes and workflows. We will also analyze a public-sector case snapshot where systems transformed accountability from a vague concept into daily practice. Finally, we will present a practical framework for supervisors to select and implement accountability tools that align with their specific context.

Section 1 — Implementing Performance Measurement Tools

Performance measurement tools provide the structure supervisors need to translate accountability into measurable outcomes. Without them, accountability conversations risk becoming subjective debates. With them, supervisors can anchor expectations in data, fairness, and transparency.

At the most basic level, performance measurement tools answer three questions:

What do we expect employees to achieve?

How will we know if they have achieved it?

How will results be reported and reviewed?

Public-sector supervisors often rely on performance scorecards, dashboards, and key performance indicators (KPIs) to evaluate their teams' performance. For example, a public health department might track vaccination rates by district, a transportation department might monitor average response times for road repairs, or a human services agency might measure the percentage of applications processed within a target timeframe. These measures create clarity for employees and provide evidence for stakeholders.

However, measurement tools must be carefully designed. Overly complex systems can overwhelm employees with paperwork, fostering resentment and hindering productivity. Metrics must be relevant, realistic, and balanced. If a police department measures only response times, officers may rush to calls without adequate preparation. Balanced scorecards, which encompass multiple dimensions such as quality, timeliness, and community satisfaction, offer a more comprehensive picture of performance.

Supervisors also need to integrate measurement tools into daily routines. A dashboard that no one checks is useless. However, when a supervisor begins each week by reviewing metrics with the team, discussing trends, and identifying opportunities for improvement, measurement becomes meaningful.

"Measurement without meaning is math. Measurement with context is accountability." — Dr. Patrick C. Patrong.

Section 2 — Using Technology to Track Progress and Maintain Transparency

Technology has transformed accountability. From digital dashboards to project management apps, supervisors now have more tools than ever to track progress and maintain transparency. The challenge is not whether tools exist, but how wisely supervisors implement them.

For public-sector teams, technology offers three significant advantages: increased visibility, enhanced efficiency, and greater transparency.

Visibility: Dashboards display progress in real time, making accountability visible to employees, supervisors, and external stakeholders. A city sanitation department might utilize GPS tracking to monitor trash collection routes, ensuring comprehensive coverage and minimizing missed pickups.

Efficiency: Project management systems streamline workflows, reducing duplication and errors. A county permitting office may use an online portal that allows residents to submit applications, track their status, and receive notifications, thereby improving accountability while reducing manual workload.

Transparency: Technology creates records that can withstand scrutiny. In environments where union grievances or political oversight are standard, digital systems provide objective evidence of performance. A human resources department that tracks employee evaluations electronically, for example, can demonstrate consistency and fairness in its processes.

Still, technology must serve people, not the other way around. Tools that are too complex or poorly integrated can overwhelm employees, creating frustration instead of clarity. Supervisors should involve staff in selecting and piloting tools, ensuring that systems enhance rather than hinder accountability.

Magic with a Message: I sometimes demonstrate a trick where multiple objects are shuffled quickly under cups, yet the ball always reappears in the same place. The audience is amazed at the consistency. The point is this: technology, when used well, ensures consistency. No matter how chaotic the environment feels, systems enable accountability to take its rightful place — visible, fair, and trackable.

Supervisors should also be mindful of privacy and trust. Employees may fear that technology is used to "spy" on them rather than to support them. Clear communication about why data is collected, how it will be used, and the benefits it provides to employees helps mitigate resistance.

"Technology is not accountability, but it makes accountability visible. Used wisely, it builds trust; used poorly, it breeds fear." — Dr. Patrick C. Patrong.

Section 3 — Developing Accountability Processes and Workflows

Tools and technology create structure, but without consistent processes and workflows, accountability quickly unravels. Processes provide the "how" — the steps by which expectations are translated into daily actions. Workflows ensure that responsibility is not left to chance but is distributed fairly and transparently across the team.

Effective accountability processes share three characteristics: they are **clear, consistent, and corrective**.

- **Clear:** Each step in the process must be documented and communicated. For example, in a public records office, the process for handling requests should define who receives them, how they are logged, timelines for response, and escalation steps if deadlines are missed.

- **Consistent:** Processes must be applied evenly. If one employee is allowed to skip steps while others are held to them, accountability erodes. Consistency builds fairness, and fairness sustains culture.

- **Corrective:** Processes must include feedback loops. When errors occur, the workflow should guide supervisors and employees toward corrective action, not just punishment. For instance, after-action reviews in emergency services ensure that lessons from mistakes are applied to future responses.

Public-sector supervisors must also ensure compliance with relevant **requirements**. Many workflows are defined by law, regulation, or contract. Supervisors cannot ignore these, but they can make them more user-friendly. Translating dense regulations into simple process maps or checklists helps employees see accountability as manageable.

Workflows should also be designed with **handoffs in mind**. Many public-sector services, from housing permits to public safety, involve multiple employees or departments. Clear handoffs reduce delays and ensure accountability is not lost in the gaps. A well-documented workflow specifies not only what each person must do but also when and how responsibility is transferred.

"Processes make accountability predictable. Without them, responsibility is left to chance; with them, it becomes a habit." — Dr. Patrick C. Patrong.

Section 4 — Public Sector Case Snapshot: The Permitting Office Overhaul

Scene 1 — Chaos at the Counter

The city's permitting office had become a source of public frustration. Contractors complained of long delays, lost paperwork, and inconsistent approvals. Citizens accused the office of favoritism. Councilmembers demanded answers. Inside the office, employees were overwhelmed and demoralized. There were no consistent workflows — each clerk had their own way of processing applications. Accountability was absent because processes were nonexistent.

Scene 2 — The Supervisor's Wake-Up Call

Luis, the new supervisor, quickly realized that the problem was not a lack of effort but a system failure. Clerks were working hard, but without a clear structure. He decided that building workflows was the only way to restore accountability and public trust.

Scene 3 — Building the Process

Luis gathered his team and mapped the permitting process step by step. They identified key stages: intake, documentation review, inspection scheduling, approval, and archiving. For each stage, they defined responsibilities, timelines, and escalation procedures. They also created standard checklists to ensure consistency. Importantly, Luis involved employees in designing the workflows, so they felt a sense of ownership rather than imposition.

Scene 4 — Embedding the Workflow

Once workflows were defined, Luis embedded them into practice. Applications were logged electronically at intake, deadlines were tracked automatically, and inspectors received digital notifications for scheduling. Weekly huddles reviewed progress and flagged bottlenecks. Accountability became visible because the process made every step traceable.

Scene 5 — Results and Recognition

Within six months, application turnaround times improved by 35 percent. Contractors reported greater confidence in the fairness of approvals. Citizen complaints declined, and councilmembers noted the improvement in public meetings. Inside the office, morale rose because employees finally felt they had a roadmap. Accountability had shifted from subjective judgment to an objective process.

Scene 6 — The Lesson

Luis later reflected, "We did not work harder; we worked differently. By creating workflows, accountability stopped being about blame and started being about progress." His story illustrates how processes and workflows transform accountability from a vague expectation into a daily habit that everyone can see and trust.

"When processes are missing, accountability feels unfair. When processes are clear, accountability feels shared." — Dr. Patrick C. Patrong.

Section 5 — Applied Tool: The Accountability Systems Checklist

Supervisors can utilize a simple yet powerful tool to determine whether their current systems effectively support accountability. I call it the Accountability Systems Checklist (ASC). It provides a structured way to evaluate tools, technology, and workflows against four criteria: clarity, consistency, transparency, and usability.

Clarity

Does the system make expectations obvious?

Example: A time-tracking system that specifies deadlines and flags overdue reports is clear and compelling. A vague memo is not.

Consistency

Is the system applied evenly across all employees?

Example: A permitting database that enforces the same workflow for every application ensures fairness. Allowing employees to invent their own processes can lead to inconsistency.

Transparency

Does the system provide visibility to both employees and supervisors?

Example: A dashboard that shows progress on city projects makes accountability visible. Hidden spreadsheets create suspicion and confusion.

Usability

Does the system help or hinder employees in their daily work?

Example: A mobile app that allows inspectors to upload reports in the field is usable. A clunky program that requires multiple logins discourages compliance.

How to Apply the ASC

1. Select one area of accountability (such as reporting, case management, or scheduling).

2. Rate your current tools on each criterion (High, Medium, Low).

3. Identify the lowest score — this is your system's weakness.

4. Design an improvement plan to strengthen that area.

Worked Example 1 — Public Safety

A fire department supervisor evaluated their incident reporting system. Clarity was high, but usability was low — the system required 45 minutes of data entry after each call. By flagging usability as a weakness, the department invested in a streamlined mobile reporting tool. The result: faster reporting, better data, and higher compliance.

Worked Example 2 — City Finance Office

The finance team utilized a budget-tracking spreadsheet that was accessible only to a select few. Transparency scored low. By shifting to a shared dashboard, everyone can see the budget status in real-time. Accountability improved because visibility was no longer limited to a few.

"Systems are only as strong as their weakest point. When supervisors assess and strengthen clarity, consistency, transparency, and usability, accountability thrives." — Dr. Patrick C. Patrong

Section 6 — Reflection Questions

Use these prompts to evaluate the effectiveness of your current accountability systems:

1. What tools currently support accountability on my team? Are they clear, consistent, transparent, and easy to use?

2. Where does accountability break down most often — at the level of measurement, technology, or workflow?

3. Do employees view systems as supportive or punitive? What message do current tools send about trust and responsibility?

4. How well do I integrate system results into daily conversations? Am I using dashboards, metrics, and reports as living tools or letting them collect dust?

5. What is one system I could simplify this month to make accountability easier for employees to practice?

Leadership-Centered Closing Summary

Tools and systems turn accountability from aspiration into practice. Performance measurement provides clarity. Technology ensures visibility and transparency. Processes and workflows make accountability predictable and fair. Together, these elements form the infrastructure that sustains long-term responsibility.

The case of Luis in the permitting office reminds us that systems do not stifle accountability — they make it possible. Employees who once felt overwhelmed and blamed became confident and consistent when workflows clarified expectations. Supervisors who once faced angry citizens found themselves presenting improved results with pride.

For public-sector supervisors, systems also provide protection. They demonstrate fairness to unions, evidence to auditors, and results to elected officials. Nevertheless, systems must be chosen carefully. Overly complex or punitive tools erode trust. The best systems support employees, simplify work, and make accountability visible to all.

"Supervisors build accountability not only through conversations but through systems that endure when conversations end." — Dr. Patrick C. Patrong.

As you move forward, evaluate your current systems with honesty and transparency. Ask whether they truly reinforce accountability or simply create noise. Simplify where possible, invest where necessary, and integrate systems into daily practice. When tools, technology, and workflows align with your leadership, accountability becomes more than a principle—it becomes a sustainable culture.

COACHING AND DEVELOPMENT FOR ACCOUNTABILITY

"Accountability is not just about correcting mistakes; it is about coaching people to grow stronger through them."

— *Dr. Patrick C. Patrong*

Introduction — Shaping Accountability Through Development

Accountability is often misunderstood as discipline. Supervisors are expected to step in when employees fall short, and the reflex is to correct or punish. Nevertheless, proper accountability is far more effective when paired with coaching and development. Supervisors who see accountability as an opportunity for growth transform mistakes into stepping stones and challenges into catalysts for improvement.

Coaching for accountability requires patience, skill, and consistency. Instead of asking, "How do I punish this mistake?" the coaching supervisor asks, "What can this moment teach us?" This approach changes the tone of accountability conversations. Employees are less likely to feel defensive and more likely to feel supported in taking ownership of their work. Over time, the culture shifts from fear of being caught to eagerness for continuous learning.

In the public sector, this approach is vital. Many employees in government service face outdated systems, limited resources, and high public expectations. Mistakes are inevitable. If accountability is purely punitive, employees will hide errors or disengage. However, when supervisors coach, employees bring problems forward, confident that the focus will be on solutions and development. The result is better service for citizens and stronger teams for agencies.

Magic with a Message: I often use the "torn and restored paper" illusion to illustrate this principle. The audience watches a piece of paper ripped into fragments, assuming it is ruined. However, then the pieces are restored, whole again. Coaching works the same way: mistakes do not have to leave permanent damage. With guidance, employees can be restored, improved, and even stronger than before.

This chapter examines how supervisors can coach employees toward accountability, offer ongoing training and development, and empower staff to take ownership of their professional growth. We will examine strategies, study a public-sector case where coaching reshaped a team, and introduce a practical tool that supervisors can use to integrate coaching into daily accountability practices.

Section 1 — Coaching Strategies to Support Growth and Accountability

Supervisors who embrace coaching as part of accountability shift the focus from fault-finding to future-building. Coaching strategies help employees see accountability not as a punishment to be endured but as a partnership that guides them toward success.

One key strategy is **asking powerful questions**. Instead of telling an employee what went wrong, supervisors can ask, "What do you think contributed to this outcome?" or "What would you do differently next time?" Questions encourage reflection, foster ownership, and prevent employees from becoming passive recipients of feedback. When employees articulate their own insights, accountability deepens.

Another strategy is **providing timely, bite-sized coaching**. Accountability conversations should not be saved for annual performance reviews. By then, issues are stale and difficult to correct. Coaching in the moment — after a missed deadline, a customer complaint, or a successful project — makes feedback relevant and actionable. Small, regular coaching conversations accumulate into long-term growth.

Supervisors should also practice **coaching through strengths**. Accountability often focuses on weaknesses, but employees improve faster when supervisors leverage their strengths. For example, suppose a caseworker struggles with time management but excels at building rapport. In that case, the supervisor can frame accountability around utilizing that rapport to streamline interviews and reduce the time spent per case. By connecting strengths to accountability, supervisors reinforce confidence and engagement.

Finally, coaching must include **modeling vulnerability**. Supervisors who share their own mistakes and what they learned send a message that accountability is universal, not just something imposed on others. A supervisor who admits, "I mishandled that meeting, and here is how I plan to improve," normalizes growth and encourages employees to embrace accountability without fear.

"Coaching for accountability is not about catching people failing; it is about catching them learning." — Dr. Patrick C. Patrong.

Section 2 — Providing Ongoing Training and Development Opportunities

Coaching is powerful, but structured opportunities for training and development must reinforce it. Accountability cannot thrive in environments where employees feel unprepared or stagnant. Supervisors who invest in development signal that accountability is not about punishment but about growth.

Training should be **practical and relevant**. Employees are more likely to embrace accountability when they see that training equips them to meet expectations. For example, if a city clerk's office introduces a new digital filing system, supervisors should ensure staff receive hands-on training rather than just a manual. When employees feel competent, they feel confident, and confidence supports accountability.

Development opportunities should also be **ongoing**, not one-time events. Public-sector employees often remain in roles for years, and initial training quickly becomes outdated. Supervisors can build development into the culture through quarterly skill refreshers, cross-training opportunities, or professional development stipends. The message is clear: learning is a continuous process, and accountability grows alongside it.

Supervisors should look for **growth beyond technical skills**. Accountability requires not only knowledge of procedures but also competencies in communication, problem-solving, and emotional intelligence. Workshops on conflict resolution or customer service, for instance, prepare employees to handle accountability situations in a constructive manner.

Importantly, development must be tied to **career progression**. Employees are more likely to embrace accountability when they see it connected to advancement. Supervisors who discuss career goals during coaching sessions, recommend employees for training aligned with those goals, and celebrate skill-building achievements create motivation for responsibility.

Magic with a Message: I sometimes demonstrate the "Professor's Nightmare" rope trick, where three ropes of different lengths become equal. Training does the same for teams. Employees start at different skill levels, but development opportunities align them to meet the same accountability standards.

"Accountability without development is discouragement. Accountability with development is empowerment." — Dr. Patrick C. Patrong

Section 3 — Empowering Employees to Take Ownership of Their Development

Genuine accountability means employees take responsibility not only for today's tasks but also for their own growth. Supervisors who empower employees to own their development move accountability beyond compliance into self-leadership.

The first step is **shifting the mindset**. Employees must see development as something they drive, not something that is done to them. Supervisors can encourage this by asking employees to identify skills they want to improve, certifications they want to pursue, or roles they aspire to. When employees set their own development goals, accountability becomes personal.

The second step is **providing tools for self-assessment**. Reflection exercises, skills inventories, and 360-degree feedback reports provide employees with data on their strengths and areas for improvement. Supervisors should guide employees in interpreting this feedback and developing action plans based on it. When employees see their own growth path clearly, they are more motivated to pursue it.

The third step is **linking development to accountability conversations**. Instead of focusing only on whether tasks were completed, supervisors can ask, "What did this project teach you about your strengths?" or "What skills do you want to build for next time?" These questions turn accountability from a backward-looking audit into a forward-looking dialogue.

Finally, empowerment requires **access to opportunities**. Supervisors should encourage employees to attend workshops, take on stretch assignments, or shadow colleagues in different roles. Even when budgets are limited, opportunities can be created through mentorship, peer learning, or rotational assignments. The key is to remove barriers so employees can act on their development goals.

"Accountability matures when employees own not just their tasks but their growth. Supervisors plant the seed, but employees must water it." — Dr. Patrick C. Patrong.

Section 4 — Public Sector Case Snapshot: The Social Services Coaching Shift

Scene 1 — A Culture of Fear

In a county social services department, caseworkers were under immense pressure. Errors in documentation could result in delayed benefits, angry clients, and negative headlines. Supervisors responded by issuing warnings and writing up employees for mistakes. Accountability was equated with discipline, and morale sank. Caseworkers began to hide errors, fearing punishment.

Scene 2 — A New Approach

When Angela became a supervisor, she chose a different path. In her first staff meeting, she acknowledged the fear and said, "Accountability does not mean punishment. It means responsibility — and responsibility includes supporting your growth. From today forward, mistakes will be treated as learning opportunities." The room was skeptical, but Angela backed up her words with action.

Scene 3 — Coaching in Action

When a caseworker missed a critical deadline, Angela resisted the urge to discipline immediately. Instead, she sat down and asked, "What got in the way?" The caseworker admitted feeling overwhelmed by the new digital case management system. Angela arranged for one-on-one coaching and paired the worker with a peer mentor. The following month, deadlines were met consistently.

Scene 4 — Building Development Routines

Angela introduced monthly coaching sessions where staff reviewed challenging cases together. Instead of pointing fingers, the team analyzed areas for improvement and shared effective strategies. She also created individual development plans, linking accountability to skill-building goals. Caseworkers began to see that accountability conversations were about progress, not punishment.

Scene 5 — Results and Recognition

Within six months, error rates dropped by 25 percent, and client satisfaction improved. Caseworkers reported higher confidence in handling complex cases. The department's reputation improved as citizens noticed faster, more accurate service. The culture had shifted: accountability was no longer a threat but a shared value tied to coaching and development.

Scene 6 — The Lesson

Angela reflected later: "We stopped treating mistakes as evidence of failure and started treating them as opportunities for coaching. That simple shift rebuilt trust and improved performance."

"Supervisors who coach through accountability turn errors into education and setbacks into growth." — Dr. Patrick C. Patrong

Section 5 — Applied Tool: The Coaching Accountability Cycle

Supervisors can integrate coaching into accountability by following a simple framework I call the **Coaching Accountability Cycle (CAC)**. This cycle ensures accountability conversations lead to growth, not fear. It includes four steps: Observe, Reflect, Guide, and Commit.

Step 1 — Observe

Supervisors begin by observing behaviors or outcomes. This step requires attentiveness. Instead of waiting until performance reviews, supervisors take note of daily actions — missed deadlines, strong customer interactions, errors in reports, or creative solutions. Observing ensures feedback is grounded in facts, not assumptions.

Step 2 — Reflect

Supervisors invite employees to reflect on the observed behavior. Questions like, "What do you think contributed to this outcome?" or "What was your thought process here?" encourage self-awareness. Reflection prevents the conversation from becoming one-sided and strengthens ownership.

Step 3 — Guide

After reflection, the supervisor provides guidance. This idea includes clarifying expectations, offering strategies, or connecting the employee with resources. Guidance should be constructive, focusing on what can be improved rather than dwelling on past mistakes.

Step 4 — Commit

The cycle ends with a commitment. The employee commits to specific actions for improvement, and the supervisor commits to providing support and guidance. This shared accountability ensures follow-through and reinforces partnership.

Worked Example 1 — Public Health Nurse

A nurse missed several documentation steps in patient records. The supervisor used the CAC. First, she observed the error factually. Then she asked the nurse to reflect, who admitted feeling rushed. The supervisor guided by reviewing a time-management strategy and was committed to adjusting schedules for fairness. The nurse is committed to consistently using the checklist. Within weeks, documentation accuracy improved.

Worked Example 2 — Public Works Crew

A crew failed to complete snow removal on time. The supervisor used CAC. He observed the missed deadline, asked the crew to reflect, and discovered that equipment breakdown was the cause. He guided the crew by arranging preventive maintenance training, and they committed to flagging mechanical issues earlier. The next storm, snow removal was completed ahead of schedule.

"Coaching makes accountability a cycle of growth, not a circle of blame."
— Dr. Patrick C. Patrang

Section 6 — Reflection Questions

These questions will help you integrate coaching into your accountability practices:

1. Do I treat accountability conversations as opportunities for growth or as moments of discipline?

Reflect on your recent conversations. What message did you send?

2. How often do I ask employees reflective questions rather than providing all the answers?

Accountability deepens when employees think critically about their own performance.

3. Do my coaching practices focus only on weaknesses, or do I leverage employee strengths?

Consider how you can tie strengths to accountability to reinforce confidence.

4. What routines have I established for ongoing development?

Are training and coaching consistent, or are they only reactive when problems occur?

5. Do I empower employees to take ownership of their growth?

What tools, opportunities, or conversations can I provide to shift development responsibility to them?

Leadership-Centered Closing Summary

Coaching and development transform accountability from a system of punishment into a process of empowerment. Supervisors who adopt coaching strategies create environments where employees feel safe to admit mistakes, reflect on their actions, and commit to improvement. Training reinforces this by equipping employees with the necessary skills to succeed. Empowerment goes even further, encouraging employees to take responsibility not only for their tasks but also for their growth.

The case of Angela in social services reminds us that accountability cultures can shift dramatically when supervisors choose coaching over discipline. What was once a culture of fear became a culture of ownership and learning. Supervisors everywhere can apply the same principles: observe, invite reflection, guide constructively, and secure commitments for improvement.

For public-sector leaders, the stakes are high. Citizens depend on competent, responsive employees. Unions and political leaders demand fairness. Coaching for accountability meets all these demands by fostering trust, enhancing performance, and sustaining morale.

Original Quote: "Supervisors who coach through accountability build not only better employees but stronger communities." — Dr. Patrick C. Patrong

"Accountability paired with coaching turns setbacks into springboards." — Dr. Patrick C. Patrong.

As you close this chapter, remember that accountability is not the end of the story — it is the beginning of growth. By coaching and developing your employees, you transform accountability from a burden into a gift. It becomes the path by which individuals, teams, and entire organizations rise to new levels of excellence.

ADDRESSING ACCOUNTABILITY CHALLENGES

"Accountability becomes most meaningful when it is tested by challenge."
— Dr. Patrick C. Patrong

Introduction — When Accountability Meets Resistance

No matter how strong a supervisor's systems, communication, or coaching practices, accountability will eventually be tested. Employees may resist standards, difficult conversations may spark conflict, or external pressures — from politics, unions, or the public — may complicate decisions. These challenges are not signs of failure; they are the proving ground of leadership.

Supervisors often wish accountability were easy — a matter of setting expectations and watching employees follow them. Nevertheless, accountability is not mechanical. It involves human emotions, competing priorities, and external scrutiny. Challenges arise because accountability requires individuals to confront uncomfortable truths about their performance, behavior, and outcomes.

In the public sector, these challenges are magnified. Supervisors operate in environments where job protections, political turnover, and limited resources can make accountability enforcement challenging. A supervisor may feel caught between upholding standards and avoiding grievances. They may struggle to hold long-serving employees accountable when cultural inertia resists change. Alternatively, they may face public criticism when accountability decisions are second-guessed by stakeholders with competing agendas.

Magic with a Message: I frequently employ the "escape from handcuffs" illusion in my training. The performer appears trapped, bound tightly, but with focus and discipline, the escape is achieved. Supervisors face similar moments when accountability challenges make them feel bound. Nevertheless, with the right tools and persistence, they can navigate the pressure and emerge stronger.

This chapter examines how supervisors can constructively address accountability challenges. We will examine strategies for overcoming resistance, managing difficult conversations and conflicts, and holding employees accountable in fair and defensible ways. We will study a case where a supervisor confronted entrenched resistance and reshaped the culture. Finally, we will provide a practical tool for navigating accountability challenges with confidence and integrity.

Section 1 — Dealing with Resistance to Accountability

Resistance to accountability is inevitable. Some employees may resist adopting standards, perceiving them as unfair or unnecessary. Others may resist because they fear exposure of weaknesses, or because past experiences have taught them that accountability means punishment. Supervisors must recognize resistance not as defiance alone, but as a signal of deeper issues.

One common form of resistance is **passive avoidance**. Employees nod in agreement during meetings but quietly continue old habits. This type of avoidance often stems from skepticism — employees doubt that accountability is genuine or that standards will be consistently enforced. The solution is persistence. Supervisors must follow through on expectations, reinforcing them consistently until employees see that accountability is more than talk.

Another form is **open pushback**. Employees may challenge the fairness of expectations, question the authority of their supervisor, or appeal to their union or HR. This resistance can feel personal, but supervisors must remain calm and professional in their approach. The key is transparency. Supervisors who can point to clear standards, documented communication, and fair processes are far more likely to withstand challenges.

Resistance can also take the form of **cultural inertia**. In long-standing organizations, employees may say, "This is how we have always done it." Change can feel threatening, and accountability is often perceived as an unnecessary disruption. Supervisors must counter inertia with vision and persistence. By demonstrating how accountability aligns with the organization's mission — serving citizens, protecting resources, or promoting fairness — supervisors can reframe accountability as a measure of progress rather than punishment.

Finally, some resistance stems from **fear**. Employees may fear losing control, failing in front of peers, or being disciplined. Supervisors can reduce fear by pairing accountability with support — offering training, coaching, and transparent processes that show accountability is about improvement, not humiliation.

"Resistance to accountability is rarely about laziness; it is about fear, habit, or mistrust. Supervisors who lead with fairness and persistence can turn resistance into resilience." — Dr. Patrick C. Patrong

Section 2 — Managing Difficult Conversations and Conflicts

Accountability challenges often crystallize in difficult conversations. These are the moments when supervisors must address underperformance, misconduct, or unmet expectations. Many supervisors dread these conversations, fearing conflict or escalation. However, avoiding them only deepens problems and erodes credibility.

Effective accountability conversations require preparation. Supervisors should enter with clear facts, specific examples, and a focus on behaviors rather than personal traits. "Your reports were late three times this month" is more effective than "You are unreliable." Facts anchor the conversation in fairness and reduce defensiveness.

Tone is equally important. A calm, respectful tone communicates professionalism, even when the message is firm—supervisors who raise their voice or show frustration risk escalating conflict. By staying composed, supervisors demonstrate that accountability is about upholding standards, not engaging in personal attacks.

Supervisors must also **listen actively** during difficult conversations. Employees often provide valuable context — such as workload imbalances, unclear instructions, or systemic barriers — that helps explain gaps. Listening does not excuse poor performance, but it does allow supervisors to address root causes. Sometimes accountability requires not only holding employees responsible but also fixing broken systems.

Conflict is not failure; it is a natural part of the accountability process. When handled constructively, conflict can strengthen relationships. For example, a heated discussion about workload can lead to a more equitable redistribution of tasks. A tense conversation about behavior can clarify expectations and prevent future issues. The key is to stay focused on outcomes: improvement, not punishment.

Magic with a Message: I sometimes use the "one ahead" illusion, where the performer appears to know a spectator's choice before it is revealed. The point is that preparation makes difficult moments easier. Supervisors who prepare for accountability conversations — gathering facts, anticipating reactions, and planning responses — enter with confidence and navigate conflict more effectively.

"Accountability conversations are not battles to be won; they are bridges to be built. When supervisors enter with clarity and respect, conflict becomes progress." — Dr. Patrick C. Patrong.

Section 3 — Strategies for Holding Employees Accountable Fairly

Fairness is the cornerstone of accountability. When employees believe they are being treated fairly, they are more willing to accept responsibility, even when the message is hard to hear. When fairness is absent, accountability can feel arbitrary and breed resentment. Supervisors must therefore approach accountability with strategies that strike a balance between firmness and equity.

The first strategy is **consistency**. Supervisors must apply standards evenly across the team. If one employee is reprimanded for tardiness while another is allowed to arrive late without consequence, the credibility of both is compromised. Consistency does not mean ignoring context — accommodations may be appropriate — but the standard must remain clear, and any exceptions must be transparent and well-documented.

The second strategy is **documentation**. Public-sector supervisors often face union grievances, political scrutiny, or legal review. Documenting expectations, conversations, and outcomes ensures accountability is defensible. Documentation also signals fairness because it demonstrates that decisions are based on evidence, rather than favoritism or emotion.

The third strategy is **progressive action**. Accountability should escalate appropriately. A first mistake may warrant coaching. Repeated issues may require formal warnings. Serious misconduct may demand disciplinary action. Progressive action demonstrates fairness by matching the response to the behavior and giving employees opportunities to improve before harsher measures are applied.

The fourth strategy is **due process**. Employees must feel they have a chance to tell their side of the story. Supervisors who listen before deciding build credibility, even if the outcome is corrective. Due process does not weaken accountability; it strengthens it by showing respect for the employee's dignity.

Finally, supervisors must practice **transparency**. Explaining the "why" behind accountability decisions reduces speculation and mistrust.

For example, if an employee is reassigned after repeated performance issues, explaining that the move is intended to match their skills better prevents rumors of bias.

Original Quote: "Fairness turns accountability from a weapon into a shield. When standards are clear and consistent, accountability protects as much as it corrects." — Dr. Patrick C. Patrong.

Section 4 — Public Sector Case Snapshot: The Veteran Employee Challenge

Scene 1 — An Entrenched Problem

In a county transportation department, Mark, a supervisor, inherited a team that included a 25-year veteran employee named Ron. Ron was well-liked by coworkers but notorious for ignoring new procedures. He frequently dismissed instructions by saying, "I have been doing this longer than you have been here." Past supervisors avoided confrontation, fearing union backlash. Accountability had eroded because no one wanted to challenge Ron.

Scene 2 — The Turning Point

When a safety audit revealed multiple violations tied to Ron's work, Mark knew he had to act. Ignoring the issue would put both staff and citizens at risk. Mark prepared carefully, gathering documentation of the violations, reviewing union guidelines, and scripting the conversation to remain respectful but firm.

Scene 3 — The Difficult Conversation

In their meeting, Mark acknowledged Ron's years of service but made expectations clear. "Your experience is valued, but safety standards apply to everyone. These violations put people at risk, and that cannot continue. I want to work with you, but accountability must be practiced." Ron pushed back, claiming the rules were unnecessary. Mark stayed calm, pointed to the audit findings, and explained the consequences of continued violations.

Scene 4 — Coaching and Consequences

Mark paired fairness with firmness. He arranged refresher training for Ron, paired him with a peer mentor, and gave him a clear improvement plan. Nevertheless, he also set boundaries: further violations would result in progressively more severe discipline. This balance signaled both support and seriousness.

Scene 5 — The Outcome

At first, Ron resisted, but over time, with coaching and consistent follow-up, he began to comply with the standards. His coworkers noticed the shift, and team morale improved because they saw accountability applied evenly, even to a veteran. The union respected Mark's process because it was documented, transparent, and fair.

Scene 6 — The Lesson

Mark later reflected, "The hardest accountability challenge is not the new employee who struggles but the long-serving one who resists. However, fairness, consistency, and documentation make even the toughest cases manageable." His experience illustrates that accountability, when handled with respect and transparency, can overcome even entrenched resistance.

"Accountability delayed is accountability denied. When supervisors finally confront long-avoided issues with fairness, they restore integrity to the whole team."
— Dr. Patrick C. Patrong.

Section 5 — Applied Tool: The Fair Accountability Framework

To navigate accountability challenges, supervisors can use a practical decision-making tool I call the **Fair Accountability Framework (FAF)**. It ensures responses to accountability issues are consistent, transparent, and defensible. The framework has four steps: Standard, Context, Action, and Follow-Up.

Step 1 — Standard

What standard or expectation was not met? Supervisors must begin by clarifying the applicable rule, policy, or performance measure that governs the situation. If the standard is vague or undocumented, accountability cannot be applied fairly and consistently.

Step 2 — Context

What factors contributed to the gap? Supervisors should investigate whether a lack of skill, a lack of motivation, unclear instructions, or systemic barriers contributed to the issue. Context shapes the fairness of the response.

Step 3 — Action

What is the appropriate response? Actions should be proportional. Coaching may be appropriate for first-time mistakes, while progressive discipline may be required for repeated or severe violations. The action must strike a balance between firmness and fairness.

Step 4 — Follow-Up

How will accountability be sustained? Supervisors must commit to follow-up conversations, documented progress checks, or further training. Without follow-up, accountability decisions lose credibility.

Worked Example 1 — Public Library Clerk

A clerk repeatedly failed to check in returned books, frustrating patrons. The supervisor used FAF. Standard: Clerks must process returns on a daily basis. Context: The clerk was covering both the desk and phone lines due to staff shortages. Action: The supervisor adjusted scheduling and coached the clerk on multitasking. Follow-Up: Weekly check-ins confirmed improvement. The issue was resolved without escalation.

Worked Example 2 — City Sanitation Driver

A driver ignored safety protocols despite repeated coaching and warnings. The supervisor applied FAF. Standard: Safety procedures are non-negotiable. Context: The driver admitted to cutting corners to save time. Action: The supervisor issued a formal warning in accordance with the organization's progressive discipline policy. Follow-Up: Inspections ensured compliance. Accountability was enforced fairly and consistently.

"Fair accountability balances standards with context. It corrects without crushing, and it disciplines without demeaning." — Dr. Patrick C. Patrong.

Section 6 — Reflection Questions

Use these prompts to consider how you respond to accountability challenges:

1. How do I typically react to resistance?

Do I avoid it, escalate quickly, or approach it with fairness and persistence?

2. When was the last time I had a difficult accountability conversation?

What worked well, and what would I handle differently now?

3. How consistent am I in applying standards across my team?

Would employees describe my approach as fair and balanced?

4. Do I document accountability processes effectively?

If challenged by a union or external review, would I be able to show fairness?

5. How do I balance support and consequence?

Do I lean too heavily on coaching without follow-through, or on discipline without development?

6. What tools, systems, or habits can I adopt to make accountability conversations less intimidating and more constructive?

Leadership-Centered Closing Summary

Accountability is tested most fiercely when resistance, conflict, and external pressures converge. Supervisors who avoid these challenges weaken trust and credibility. Supervisors who confront them with fairness, consistency, and transparency strengthen not only their teams but also the institutions they serve.

This chapter explored strategies for managing resistance, conducting difficult conversations, and applying accountability fairly. We examined the story of Mark and Ron, which showed that even entrenched resistance can be overcome with documentation, due process, and persistence. We also introduced the Fair Accountability Framework, a practical tool supervisors can use to respond to accountability challenges with confidence and integrity.

For public-sector leaders, accountability challenges are unavoidable. Political scrutiny, union protections, and public expectations create pressure from every side. Yet these challenges also present opportunities. Each difficult conversation, each fair decision, each consistent standard strengthens the culture of accountability.

"Supervisors who face challenges with fairness transform obstacles into opportunities to demonstrate integrity." — Dr. Patrick C. Patrong.

As you close this chapter, remember: challenges do not weaken accountability — they define it. When supervisors respond with courage, fairness, and persistence, accountability becomes more than a concept. It becomes a lived reality that employees respect, citizens trust, and organizations depend upon.

Conclusion — The Transformative Power of Accountability

"Accountability is not the end of leadership — it is the essence of it." — Dr. Patrick C. Patrong.

Recap — The Journey Through Accountability

Throughout this book, we have walked together through the various dimensions of accountability. We began with the foundation, clarifying that accountability is not about blame but about responsibility. We explored the mindset shift required to transition from fear to ownership, and examined how clarity, communication, and culture contribute to sustainable accountability. We studied how tools, coaching, and fair processes reinforce accountability, and we confronted the reality of challenges that test supervisors' resolve.

The message has been consistent: accountability is not a one-time event or a tool of punishment. It is a way of thinking, a way of leading, and a way of building trust. For supervisors in state and municipal organizations — where scrutiny is high, resources are tight, and stakes are significant — accountability is not optional. It is the thread that weaves fairness, performance, and public trust together.

Accountability as Leadership Integrity

At its core, accountability is integrity lived out loud. It is the supervisor's responsibility to model the responsibility they expect from their teams. It is fairness applied consistently, communication practiced openly, and support offered generously. When supervisors embrace accountability as a matter of integrity, they move beyond compliance to credibility. They become leaders whom employees respect and citizens trust.

The Ongoing Work of Accountability

Accountability is never finished. Each new project, each new challenge, each new employee brings opportunities to reinforce or weaken accountability. The habits you build — setting clear expectations, coaching constructively, listening actively, documenting fairly, and celebrating responsibility — are the practices that sustain accountability over time.

"Accountability is not a destination. It is a daily discipline." — Dr. Patrick C. Patrong.

Action Plan — Steps to Lead with Accountability

As you close this book, take these actions to embed accountability into your leadership:

1. **Model Responsibility:** Hold yourself accountable first. Admit mistakes, own outcomes, and set the standard.

2. **Set Clarity:** Define expectations in writing. Ensure they are specific, measurable, and reinforced regularly.

3. **Communicate Constantly:** Practice two-way communication. Ask employees to restate expectations, and listen actively.

4. **Coach for Growth:** Use accountability conversations as coaching opportunities. Focus on learning and development, not just correction.

5. **Build Culture:** Shape daily experiences, beliefs, and behaviors that reinforce accountability. Recognize and reward ownership.

6. **Leverage Systems:** Utilize tools, technology, and workflows that make accountability transparent, equitable, and sustainable.

7. **Face Challenges:** Address resistance directly, fairly, and consistently. Document your actions, respect due process, and persist in your efforts.

Original Quote: "Accountability endures when supervisors build systems, shape culture, and live the responsibility they ask of others." — Dr. Patrick C. Patrong.

Closing Thought

Accountability is not a burden to be feared but a gift to be embraced. It fosters fairness, builds trust, enhances performance, and upholds the public trust that government supervisors uphold every day. As you move forward, commit to being the kind of leader who embraces accountability not as a requirement but as a calling. When you do, you will not only transform your team but also contribute to stronger communities and more trusted institutions.

ABOUT THE AUTHOR

Dr. Patrick C. Patrong is an accomplished leader, consultant, and speaker with over 30 years of experience transforming organizations through people-centered leadership. He is currently engaged as the Assistant Deputy Director for Human Resources Strategic Initiatives at the Virginia Museum of Fine Arts. He is President of Patrong Enterprises Inc., a firm dedicated to leadership development, organizational growth, and employee empowerment.

A graduate of multiple executive leadership academies and a certified Lean Six Sigma Black Belt, Dr. Patrong holds a Doctorate in Strategic Leadership. His philosophy centers on creating opportunity-driven cultures where supervisors are equipped to inspire growth, build trust, and lead with integrity.

Known for his engaging "Magic with a Message" teaching style, Dr. Patrong blends practical insight with memorable storytelling and interactive demonstrations. His work spans public sector agencies, universities, and cultural institutions, where he has guided leaders through change, coached teams toward resilience, and developed innovative leadership programs, including the Supervisory Learning Experience (SLE) and the PAAL™ system (Posture, Attire, Attitude, and Language).

Beyond his professional achievements, Dr. Patrong is a photographer, mentor, and creative entrepreneur who integrates his cultural heritage and artistic vision into his leadership approach. His lifelong commitment is summed up in the guiding principle of his firm: "Transforming Organizations – One Employee at a Time!

www.ingramcontent.com/pod-product-compliance
Lightning Source LLC
Chambersburg PA
CBHW070000100426
42741CB00012B/3095